Ancient Greek, Roman & Byzantine Costume

MARY G. HOUSTON

DOVER PUBLICATIONS, INC.
Mineola, New York

Bibliographical Note

This Dover edition, first published in 2003, is an unabridged republication of the second edition of the work, originally published as Volume II of the series "A Technical History of Costume" by Adam & Charles Black, Ltd., London, in 1947 under the title *Ancient Greek, Roman and Byzantine Costume and Decoration* (first publication: 1931). The eight original color plates have been reproduced in black and white in their original positions in the book. Plates II and VII appear in color on the inside front and back covers, respectively.

Library of Congress Cataloging-in-Publication Data

Houston, Mary G. (Mary Galway), b. 1871.
 Ancient Greek, Roman & Byzantine Costume / Mary G. Houston.
  p. cm.
 Includes bibliographical references and index.
 ISBN 0-486-42610-6 (pbk.)
  1. Costume—Rome—History. 2. Costume—Greece—History. 3. Costume—Byzantine Empire—History. 4. Rome—Civilization. 5. Greece—Civilization—To 146 B.C. 6. Byzantine Empire—Civilization—1081–1453. I. Title: Ancient Greek, Roman, and Byzantine costume. II. Title.

GT555.H68 2003
391—dc21

2003043781

Manufactured in the United States of America
Dover Publications, Inc., 31 East 2nd Street, Mineola, N.Y. 11501

INTRODUCTION

IF this work is to be kept within its limitations, it is naturally impossible to give a complete survey of all the varieties of the various styles. To get this knowledge it will be necessary to consult the works of reference of which lists are given in the bibliography at the end. On the other hand, the author has endeavoured to give the fullest information on the *construction* of costume as, without this knowledge, it cannot even be correctly drawn much less reproduced upon the stage.

Recent archaeological discoveries have been taken advantage of in the present volume, as in the case of Cretan costume, a style which has necessarily not been described in histories of an earlier date.

Every costume given has been actually cut out and made up before being illustrated, except in a few cases which are of the nature of duplicates, so that by following the directions given it will be easy for anyone to reproduce them in material. Where decoration is required, the exact drawing and colouring of the various styles of Historic Ornament will enable such details to be appropriately applied.

Throughout the book, the illustrations are given by means of facsimiles of drawings by artists of the various centuries, so that a historic survey of the History of Figure Drawing is here seen ; though where the drawings of primitive artists do not clearly express the ideas intended to be conveyed, a modern drawing of the garment on a lay figure is used for explanation of the measured drawings of the cut-out garments. Special care has been taken to give a thoroughly comprehensive explanation of the various elaborate arrangements of the toga, after the second century A.D., as these are draperies about which it has hitherto been extremely difficult to obtain definite information.

The large number of illustrations in the Greek section of this book, showing as they do with what variety and beauty the changes can be rung on two simple themes, *i.e.* the T-shaped tunic and rectangular shawl, will make the present volume a convenient form of inspiration for designers who may wish to produce variants within a style : also, where more exact reproduction is needed, as in theatrical work, pageantry and so forth, the careful working out of the details of cut and decoration will expedite production especially when a good reference library is not accessible.

To the Art Student, in addition to the always interesting history of costume, the development of the Art of Representation, as shown in the illustrations of these volumes, which is so strangely repeated in the personal history of every young person learning to draw, should be attractive and instructive. Finally, in connection with the history lesson in the ordinary school, it is suggested that teachers will find the illustrations clear and helpful, especially if dramatic representations are attempted.

NOTE ON THE SECOND EDITION

SINCE the publication of the first edition of this volume I have had greater leisure for study and this has enabled me to amplify considerably the original work.

I feel that thanks are specially due to the authorities at The Victoria and Albert Museum, The Greek Church of S. Sophia, London, and The Linenhall Library, Belfast, Northern Ireland, for the facilities afforded me in my researches.

MARY G. HOUSTON

January 1946

CONTENTS

FULL-PAGE PLATES

IN COLOUR*

IN BLACK AND WHITE
OVER TWO HUNDRED FIGURES IN PEN
AND INK THROUGHOUT THE TEXT

* For the Dover edition, the eight color plates are printed in black and white within the text. Plates II and VII appear in color on the inside front and back covers, respectively.

WOMAN TOREADOR
(See pp. 18 and 20.)

ANCIENT GREEK, ROMAN & BYZANTINE COSTUME

CHAPTER I

AEGEAN COSTUME

THE term Aegean is now used to describe that civilization which had its fountain-head in Crete and its latest development on the Greek mainland. The period here covered is *c.* 2100 B.C. till 1100 B.C. The Palace of Minos, at Knossos, in Crete and the ancient City of Mycenae on the Greek mainland have given rise to the words Minoan and Mycenaean, as the great wealth of archaeological discovery yielded up by these two sites justifies the usage. Sir A. Evans has divided Aegean civilization into three periods and has laid down the dates for each as follows : " Early Minoan " 3400 B.C.–2100 B.C., " Middle Minoan " 2100 B.C.–1580 B.C., and " Late Minoan," which includes Mycenaean, at 1580 B.C.–1100 B.C. He relates the above three periods to some extent with the periods of the " Old," "Middle" and commencement of the " New Kingdom " in Egypt. (Dating —Old Kingdom 3400 B.C., Middle *c.* 2375 B.C., and New 1580 B.C.–610 B.C. See *Cambridge Ancient History*.)

The costume of Minoan Crete and of Mycenaean Greece has now become almost as familiar to us as that of Ancient

Egypt and Assyria, but until some sixty odd years ago the
very existence of the brilliant civilization, of which it is a
part, was hidden from mankind. The discoveries of Schliemann at Mycenae and near-by Tiryns and later those of
Sir A. Evans and others in Crete held perhaps the greatest
archaeological surprise the world had so far known. It was,
indeed, the light thrown on Aegean costume, more especially that of the women, which gave most cause for astonish-
ment. Hitherto the simple draperies of the ancient Egyptians
and Assyrians led us to imagine that these and none other
were the garments of the ancient world—when, therefore,
there emerged the earlier Minoan ladies wearing costumes
apparently distended by crinolines and their descendants
of the later Minoan and Mycenaean Periods in tight-fitting
jackets and flounced skirts, all previous conceptions as to
the dress of this remote period were dissipated. The origin
of this elaborate style of costume must be assigned in the
main to the island of Crete itself but there are influences
from the outside world which cannot be ignored. Professor
Childe in his book *The Most Ancient East* tells us that on the
walls of prehistoric Spanish cave-shelters there are drawings
which show women who are wearing " bell-shaped skirts."
Again in the matter of flounces the same authority cites the
" kaunakes " as a woollen material where the threads of the
web hang down in loops giving the appearance of flounces.
This flounced material was characteristic of the costume of
the ancient Sumerians and is considered to have been
originally made from the skin of a sheep with the fleece
left on ; afterwards this was imitated in weaving. In Mesopotamian lands it survived as the costume of the gods after
ordinary men and women had taken to plain woven
draperies, and it is very frequently seen on cylinder-seals from

Mesopotamia where gods are represented. Small objects like seals are easily transported, and some of them having travelled to Crete (one found at Platanos in Crete shows a costume similar to Fig. 2 dating *c*. 2000 B.C.) would suggest the idea of flounces for the dress of persons of distinction. It will be of interest to compare two examples of Mesopotamian costume with an early Aegean illustration. Fig. 1 is from a bas-relief which is now in the Louvre and which has been dated *c*. 2900 B.C. Here Ur-Nina, Patesi (High Priest) of Lagash, is represented with his

Fig. 1.

family. Fig. 1, said by one authority (Waddell) to be his daughter " Lidda " and by another (Rostovtzeff) to be his prime minister " Dudu," is wearing the characteristic Sumerian skirt, which in this early example may be of actual sheepskin ; there is an extra wrap covering one shoulder. Fig. 2 is from a Mesopotamian seal-impression (*c*. 2000 B.C.). It represents a minor goddess, and in this case the costume is the " kaunakes " woven woollen stuff with flounced effect. Here the smaller shawl entirely covers the upper part of the body with the exception of the right shoulder. Fig. 3 shows a woman wearing a flounced cloak with one arm free. This is a betrothal scene from an ivory cylinder found near

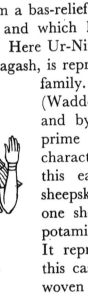

Fig. 2.

Fig. 3.

Knossos and is of early Middle Minoan period (*c.* 2100 B.C.). It can be noted here that the male figure is nude except for a belt (to which a dagger is attached) and a sheath which depends from the belt in front. (Owing to the lack of detail in the original the belt has been supplied from another early Minoan figure of the same date.) It is almost unavoidable, when describing Minoan costume, to refrain from giving that of the women prominence of place owing to the fact that in the earlier periods Minoan men were almost nude, and even in the later epochs, except on some occasions of ceremony, wore only a small kilt or abbreviated apron depending from the waist-belt back and front.

STYLE I.

Before dismissing the subject of foreign influence on Minoan styles the proximity of the ancient civilization of Egypt to that of Crete must not be overlooked. At a very early period in Egyptian history we find that a cloak enveloping the whole figure was not unusual as an article of dress, and it has been suggested that this may have been the origin of certain costumes found at Petsofa in Crete, which illustrate the first definite style of Minoan costume and are of the early Middle Minoan Period. Sir A. Evans considers that a long cloak, as worn by Cretan women, was cut out

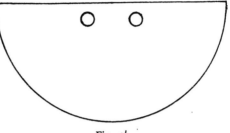

Fig. 4b.

"after the manner of a cope" (compare Etruscan semi-circular "toga"). A girdle was passed round the waist over the cloak and knotted in front; also holes were cut to allow the arms to emerge. Fig. 4a is a drawing made from an artist's lay figure upon which a cloak, cut out on the plan of a cope, has been draped after the manner suggested by Sir A. Evans. In the above sketch the drapery used for this "cope" or cloak was a thick cotton poplin material (such as is customarily used for window curtains) and the miniature lay-figure was a little over one foot in height. If an ·actual woman of average height were draped in a cloak made from either thick woollen felted cloth or from leather, the effect would be similar and there would be no need to distend the bottom of the garment with a crinoline· or hoop. Fig. 4b shows the cloak as a flat pattern; its diameter would, of course, depend on the height of the wearer. Fig. 5 is from a statuette found at Petsofa and of early Middle Minoan Period. Here we have a costume possibly cut on the lines of Figs. 4a and b or perhaps developed

Fig. 4a.

Fig. 5.

from that into a fitted bodice with skirt
attached, which latter is either cut with
gores narrowing at the waist or gathered
into it. There is also a striped decoration
upon the skirt which has the appearance
of appliqué work. This, if of leather,
would certainly help to stiffen it and so
assist the crinoline-like silhouette. The
" Medici collar " effect at the back of the
neck is seen also in Fig. 4a and is the
result of the " cope-like " cutting out.
The padded and knotted girdle somewhat
resembles that of the " Snake Goddess "
at Figs. 7d and e though in the latter case
the waist is encircled with actual snakes.
The hat of Fig. 5 swells outwards over the
ears and when viewed from the front is
not unlike a certain type of European head-
dress of the fifteenth century A.D. This
figure should be compared with the highly
ornamented " votive " skirt of later date
shown at Fig. 29a. Here is an instance of
the older fashion surviving as a sacred
garment ; so, for example, the costume of
the thirteenth century A.D. has remained
in use as the almost universal dress of sacred
personages as represented in European
Christian art. Fig. 6 is a male costume
contemporaneous with Fig. 5, if indeed it
can be called a costume at all, when so near
to absolute nudity. This man wears, in
front, a leather sheath such as was worn in

Fig. 6.

predynastic Egypt and in Libya and over it a small loin-cloth of indefinite shape which may be of leather also or possibly wool or linen (it is painted white on the statuette like the boots). A dagger is attached in front of waist and high white leather boots are worn as in present-day Crete. The small disc-like cap or hat has been added from another example.

Style II.

We now come to the more elaborate women's costumes of the later style (which developed towards the end of the Middle Minoan Period); this shows a change in the silhouette of the skirt, which fits fairly tightly down to the knees and then develops a slight flare at the bottom. Most, but not all of these skirts are flounced and the tightly fitting bodices show clearly-marked seams indicating a highly developed school of dressmaking in which there are several methods used to achieve the desired fitting. It is difficult to resist speculation as to what induced the Minoan dressmakers to attempt their elaborate effects and again to try to put forward a theory as to how they succeeded in carrying out their ideas with such distinction. The Mesopotamian " kaunakes " costume from imported seals gives an answer to *why* these flounced skirts appeared, and possibly the answer as to how the bodices were fitted with such success lies in the suggestion that the first material dealt with by these workers was *leather*, not woven material ; then, when the style was developed, the effects achieved by the use of a medium easy to cut, and lending itself to moulding the figure, such as leather undoubtedly is, give the answer as to *how* the style was formed in the first place. We must also recall the fact that the Cretans were already skilled workers in leather. The Minoan warrior carried a shield covered with bull's hide, he had high leather boots and the wearing of leather skirts or aprons was common to both priests and priestesses at certain religious ceremonies (*see* Fig. 13, p. 15). It can be said that, in costume, the idea of fitting as opposed to draping seems to be connected with the use of leather; one has only to recall the tightly fitting tunics and the trousers of the ancient Persians, Phrygians and Scythians as opposed to the floating draperies of the ancient Egyptians and Greeks to recognize this fact. Besides the flounced and flared skirt and the elaborately cut, tight-fitting bodice which characterized the Minoan women's dress of this period we find the belt always an important feature. This covers the joining of bodice and skirt. It is sometimes padded, at other times made apparently of metal and curved to the figure. In addition there is a third garment which was often worn over the skirt which took the form of an apron back and front and was apparently borrowed from male costume. This double apron was not, however, of universal wear and has, possibly, some religious significance. The head-dress, when worn, seems to have been either a tall tiara in three tiers or a species of round hat widening at the crown and greatly resembling in silhouette the Scottish tam-o'-shanter. This flat-crowned hat had also points in common with certain Hittite examples and even with that Persian cap called by the Greeks the " mitra." Indeed the tall tiara had also its prototype in Hittite costume. Shoes or sandals were, in Crete, essentially for outdoor wear, naked feet with possibly anklets were worn indoors. As will be seen from the illustrations the costumes of this era were lavishly decorated, the ornament thereon having generally the appearance of embroidery. Certain types of pattern, however, suggest

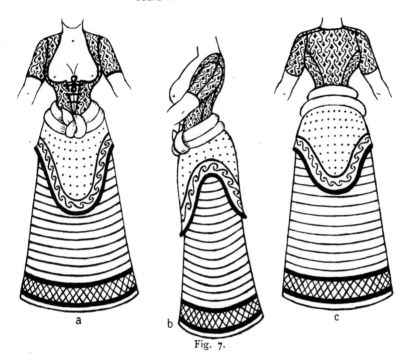

Fig. 7.

weaving, and in some cases small metal plaques may have been used as a sort of appliqué.

Figs. 7*a*, *b* and *c*, is a diagrammatic rendering of the well-known faience statuette called the " Snake Goddess " from Knossos. This is now in the Candia Museum but the British Museum possesses a replica. The date is of the latest Middle Minoan period and from this period onwards the style here shown becomes stereotyped in its main features until the fall of Aegean civilization at the end of the twelfth century B.C. The main features of this dress with its bodice, skirt and curious double-apron are described on p. 10, but Figs. 7*d* and 7*e* show the head-dress in back and front views, the hairdressing and the three live snakes coiling

Fig. 7d.   Fig. 8.   Fig. 7e.

over the body of the goddess, which have been omitted from
Figs. 7a, b and c in order to show clearly the method of
seaming on the tight-fitting bodice. Plate I. is a free drawing
from the companion statuette to Fig. 7. This has been called
the " Votary " or Priestess to the Snake Goddess. (The
statuette is practically in monochrome ; Plate I. is coloured
after a contemporary fresco). Here we are introduced to
the flounced skirt and flat tam-o'-shanter shaped hat each
so characteristic of this later style. The flounces of this skirt
have the appearance of being pleated and the tam-o'-shanter
hat is decorated with ornamental discs, also at Fig. 8, which
is a front view of Plate I., we see perched on the top of the
hat an animal which resembles a miniature leopard or other

spotted creature; this has been omitted from Plate I. for lack of space. A contemporary male costume is shown at Fig. 9—the well-known " Cup-bearer of Knossos " (Candia Museum). Unlike the two previous women's costumes, the dress at Fig. 9 is a style which did not long survive and may be said to have disappeared early in the Late Minoan Period. This is, no doubt, due to the fact that it is most probably a foreign importation either from Western Asia or from Egypt. The youth here represented is probably of noble birth, one who served as a page in the royal palace. He wears no sandals, being in indoor dress. A noteworthy feature of this figure is the pinched-in waist, this peculiarity was not confined to the Minoan women of the close of the Middle and throughout

Fig. 9.

the Late Minoan Periods. The men, by means of their tight metal belts, were even more successful in compressing this portion of the body and gave the impression of being almost ready to break in two at the waist. This peculiarity is also in evidence when we come to examine Mycenaean male costumes, as will be seen at Figs. 23 and 25. A very interesting sidelight on the costumes of the Cup-bearer type is seen in the representation from an eighteenth-dynasty Egyptian tomb at Thebes of a procession of foreign envoys carrying gifts and called by the Egyptians " Men of the Keftiu " or

Fig. 10.

"Men of the Isles." These men, with their long hair arranged in characteristic Minoan fashion and with kilts recalling that of the Cup-bearer, show this costume as seen by a foreign artist. Fig. 10 shows this Egyptian drawing. Here sandals are worn as part of outdoor dress and it is interesting to note that sandals of almost identical design have been found on an ivory statuette from Crete. As has been said this almost knee-length kilt was not in wear for any considerable period and it may be considered as a court-dress of the close of the Middle Minoan Age. Both previous to and after the age of the long kilt, the truly characteristic Minoan male costume was the double-apron depending from a tight belt. At the back the apron usually reached more than half-way down the thigh, but in front it was shorter, often only just covering the leather sheath (which was generally worn underneath it) or at times it was worn a few inches longer than the sheath. Fig. 11 shows the costume of a young prince or chieftain. It is part of a bas-relief decoration of a vase found at Hagia Triada in Crete and is an example of male costume of the Late Minoan Period; here the long hair in its arrangement differs little from that

of Figs. 9 and 10. In this case the
sandals have developed into puttees,
but the long kilt has disappeared and
in its stead we have the double-apron
slightly longer at the back than in
the front. A dagger is thrust into
the belt and the deep jewelled collar
is almost as massive as that worn by
the ancient Egyptians. Fig. 12 is a
restoration of the costume worn by a
king or prince of the commencement
of the Late Minoan Era—the original
is in the museum at Candia and repro-
ductions are installed in other museums,
as, for example, at Oxford. Here we
have the typical loin-covering of the

Fig. 11.

Minoans. The tight metal belt seems to be padded inside
and the double-apron reaches half-way down the thigh at
the back, but in front it merely covers the leather sheath
which is evidently present underneath. The patterning on
this apron is from another fresco and the sandals come from
an ivory statuette of the Late Minoan Period—the head-
dress is specially important. It is of the same silhouette as
that worn by the Votary (see Plate I. and Fig. 8). Instead of
the rosettes shown at Fig. 8 we have a row of lilies with
innumerable stamens projecting (the flower is considered
by some authorities to be a combination of the lily with that
Egyptian flowering-rush called the "papyrus"). From the
crown projects another lily, from which, in turn, there
emerge three long peacock's feathers. This head-dress, in
a simple form, is seen in wear at Fig. 14, which represents a
woman assisting at a funeral or commemoration service.

Fig. 12.

Fig. 13.   Fig. 14.   Fig. 15.

In the Minoan representations of the sphinx, the head,
usually that of a female, is adorned with a plumed head-dress
similar to that of Fig. 12. In Fig. 13, which is from the celebrated painted sarcophagus found at Hagia Triada in Crete
and now in the Candia Museum, we see the costume of a
priestess standing before an altar. She wears an apron made
of the skin of an animal and in addition, the short tight-
fitting jacket which has been already illustrated at Fig. 7
and Plate I. On the same sarcophagus there are figures of
priests clad in aprons of identical shape, but in this case the
bodies are nude from the waist up. Fig. 14, again from the
sarcophagus, is wearing the long straight-cut tunic com-
monly seen in Mesopotamia and Asia Minor from very early
times. This garment when spread out flatly takes the shape
of the letter " T." The neck-hole is frequently cut as a circle

fitting the neck, and with a small vertical slit of about 5 inches over the chest to allow for the entry of the head, the top of the slit being tied together with tasselled cords. This arrangement of the neck is seen in Palestine but further north the Greek colonists in Asia Minor cut the neck opening as a horizontal slit, long enough to admit the head (*see* "Ionic" costume, p.52). In Fig. 14 the neck-hole is cut after the Ionic manner, as a slit, and the seams of the whole garment are strengthened by bands of what is, most probably, woven wool tapestry. This illustration shows that, though the tight bodice and flounced skirt was pre-eminently the dress of Minoan women of fashion from the late Middle Minoan Period till the fall of

Fig. 16.

Knossos, what is called " The Mainland Dress " was not unknown, though it seems to have been worn by both sexes as a garment of ceremony, religious or otherwise. When worn by men it was identical in shape with that worn by women. Fig. 15 shows a youthful spearman clad in a shorter tunic of identical cut; this is inserted here for purposes of comparison with Fig. 14. Fig. 15 is actually from the Greek mainland and has its place along with Fig. 26 on p. 24, where the youth holding a hound in leash wears a similar tunic. Fig. 16 is a musician from the Hagia Triada sarcophagus who wears the Mainland tunic identical in shape with that of Fig. 14. He plays on a seven-stringed lyre. Another male musician, again wearing the long tunic, plays the double pipes in the same procession. These three figures,

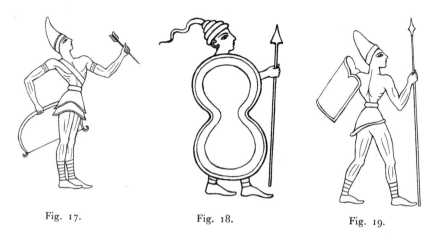

Fig. 17.   Fig. 18.   Fig. 19.

i.e. Figs. 14, 16 and the above-mentioned flute-player belong
to the latest period, namely, end of the Late Minoan. There
is little of the nature of armour seen in representations of
Minoan warriors. The body was protected by a large
"man-covering" shield; Figs. 17, 18 and 19 are from Minoan
seals, the originals being on a very small scale. There is little
or no detail but here we see three
warriors, Figs. 17 and 19 wearing
peaked caps. Fig. 17 has a kilt with
a double flounce and a baldric for
his quiver of arrows. Fig. 19, a
spearman, has a shield, curved in
section, and ending at the top in a
species of triple arch. Fig. 18 has
the typical figure-of-eight Minoan
shield and his head is protected by a
type of helmet which seems to be
made of rings of padded leather. Fig.
20 is a boxer clad in a typical Late

Fig. 20.

Minoan double-apron, helmet with cheek-pieces, and boots with leather puttees. This is from a vase known as " The Boxer Vase " (early Late Minoan) decorated with figures of men and bulls in relief. It was discovered at Hagia Triada. The so-called " Harvester Vase " *c.* 1600 B.C., also decorated with reliefs, shows men returning from the harvest field, in procession, clad in the same costume but wearing also either a turban-like cap or beret (compare Fig. 6) or, as some authorities think, having their hair wound round their heads. The leader of the procession is enveloped in a cloak covered with large scales. The representation is not, however, very clear, so that the cutting out of this cloak cannot be determined. Fishermen wear a very short kilt and no boots, which, in their case, would of course be in the way of their work. One can hazard the assumption that working-class women may have been dressed in the cloak-derived costume shown at Fig. 5 or even in the cloak itself with a girdle as shown at Fig. 4 or in a very simple plain skirt. It would certainly be difficult to imagine any one but a lady of fashion clad in the elaborately flounced dresses already described. For working women the head-dress, if worn, would have probably been the round flat cap or beret as worn by the man at Fig. 6, as an early seal-impression shows. Fig. 21 is a reconstructed drawing from Late Minoan examples of the figure of a dancer. It will be seen that, in addition to the short tight bodice, she wears a transparent vest covering the breast, otherwise her costume is similar to that of Plate I. except for the important fact that she does not wear the double-apron as seen on the Snake Goddess and her Votary ; her costume in fact is that of the typical fashionable lady of the end of the Middle Minoan and the beginning of Late Minoan Periods. The illustration facing p. 1, shows the

Fig. 21.

figure of a woman toreador. In these feats of skill and daring
the youth of Crete, men and women alike, were dressed in
the male costume of double-apron, short in front and long
behind, boots were worn to protect the feet when jumping
and the hair was left flying free—there is little to distinguish
the sex of these young figures except the colouring. In all
Minoan coloured frescoes the skin of the women is rendered
in white while that of the men is coloured brownish red ;
we notice a similar convention in Ancient Egypt. The
drawing is a reconstruction from representations of several
incomplete figures in a fresco dating *c.* 1500 B.C.

STYLE III.

Mycenaean Costume. The women's dress is really
identical with that of the Late Minoan. The silhouette is
practically the same as that of the end of the Middle Minoan
Period, but the Late Minoan and Mycenaean skirt underwent
a slight modification in its detail. Here we see the flounces
cut with a dipping peak in back and front, also, as a rule,
the foundation skirt shows in places, the flounces being
placed at intervals. Some authorities speak of the *divided
skirt* of very Late Minoan and of Mycenaean styles, but
others consider that the impression of division is merely due
to the contemporary artist's difficulty in representing the
undulating hem of a wide skirt not supported by a crinoline.
There is this to be said for the latter theory, namely, that in
the same picture (as, for example, in a certain seal-impression) the figures of women represented in three-quarter
and full front view wear what seem to be wide flounced
trousers in the one case and a skirt in the other, yet both
these garments are identical in silhouette and detail. The

Fig. 22.

balance of opinion is distinctly
against the idea that the skirt
was divided. Fig. 22 is the figure
of a woman from a processional
fresco from Tiryns near Mycenae.
Here we see the peaked flounces
dipping downwards and a
drawing which gives the idea of
a divided skirt but is probably
indicated thus to give the idea of
undulation. The long elaborately dressed hair surpasses any
of the examples yet given in its
flamboyant luxuriance. It is
possible that the border decora-

Fig. 23.

tion on this bodice may be of thin golden appliqués—the
skirt appears to be embroidered and possibly, in the case of
some of the flounces, to be pleated. A very similar figure has
been found at near-by Thebes in Boeotia. In this case the
flounces are fewer and do not commence till about eleven
inches below the waist when we get three narrow flounces, one
wide, and again three narrow and so reaching to the hem.

Fig. 24.

Fig. 25.

Figs. 23, 24 and 25 are from seals, hence detail is lacking, though the drawings are of interest from the point of view of costume. Figs. 23 and 25 found at Mycenae and Thisbe respectively draw our attention to the fact that while the women of Mycenae and the neighbouring cities adopted the Minoan fashion without reserve their male contemporaries wore, instead of the kilt or apron, a pair of short drawers and also, in some cases, the upper part of the body is covered by a vest as at Fig. 25. Fig. 23, a warrior from a Mycenaean seal-impression, shows a helmet similar in type to that of Fig. 18, namely, one made of rows of padded leather sewn together and with a horse-hair plume issuing from the top. He has the pinched-in waist of the Minoan men but the short drawers decorated with tassels are typically Mycenaean. Another warrior from the same seal carries a shield with curved or semi-cylindrical section and triple-arched top, larger though otherwise similar to that of Fig. 19. Fig. 24 shows an adaptation of the Minoan skirt to the costume of a huntress ; like the Greek Artemis, she is pursuing the stag. Her short bodice, of which we see the back view, is crossed by a baldric attached to her quiver, the skirt is not flounced but is covered with embroidered decorations. She wears boots apparently, but the detail here is lacking. Like Fig. 25 this " golden bead-seal " was discovered at Thisbe in Boeotia and dates early fifteenth century B.C. Fig. 25 is from a similar seal, the subject of which is the youthful prince Oedipus engaged in slaying the sphinx. Here the upper part of the body is covered by a tight vest or tunic, and below a pair of short drawers like those of Fig. 23 completes the costume. The whole is edged with tassels or pendants. These may be of metal as also may be the decorative spotting seen on vest and drawers. Fig. 26 in what has been referred to as

Fig. 26.

Mainland dress, is from a fresco at Tiryns. This costume is identical with that already illustrated at Fig. 15. The subject of this fresco, which belongs to the latest phase of Aegean art, is that of a number of persons starting for the hunt. Two youthful figures in a chariot who are also of the hunting-party wear ankle-length tunics practically identical with that of the woman carrying a yoke and the lyre-player from the Minoan-painted Sarcophagus at Hagia Triada (*see* Figs. 14 and 15). Fig. 27 is from a fresco at Mycenae and shows a man in Mainland dress wearing a helmet with cheek-pieces. This was probably of leather and these helmets were often sewn over with rows of boars' tusks as an added protection. The tunic here is practically identical with that of Figs. 15 and 26. Fig. 28 is from the blade of an inlaid dagger found at Mycenae and dating *c.* 1600 B.C. This represents five youthful warriors (of whom only three are shown in the drawing) engaged in hunting the lion. Detail is lacking in this extraordinarily spirited presentation of the subject but it is interesting, besides showing the typical Mycenaean short drawers as worn at this date, for the reason that the complete picture has three types of shield used simultaneously. As will be seen the two shown at Fig. 28 are figure-of-eight and rectangular in shape respectively.

Fig. 27.

Fig. 28.

Besides these there is another figure-of-eight which seems to
be semi-cylindrical in section and a fourth example which
has the arched top seen at Fig. 19. It should be noted that
in Fig. 28 the bowman carries no shield, these were used
by spearmen only. Finally, to sum up these styles as illustrated in Chapter I., we have seen that the dress of the
women shows three types, the latest of which was common
both to Minoan and Mycenaean costumes, while in that of
the men the primitive Minoan loin-cloth, the (almost) knee-
length kilt and the double-apron were pre-eminently Minoan,
their place being taken in Mycenaean men's dress by short
drawers. Again what has been called Mainland dress
was worn in its ankle-length form by both sexes in Minoan
and Mycenaean styles alike and as a shorter tunic by Mycenaean men, remembering always that this tunic, long or
short, was of almost world-wide wear.

AEGEAN ORNAMENT

The amazing beauty and variety of Aegean ornament
can only be realized after a careful study of the immense

quantity of examples which have been unearthed. Both from the island of Crete itself, from Tiryns and other sites in Greece, from Cyprus and from Rhodes, we get a profusion of fragments showing a fertility of design, a sense of fitness, and at the same time a feeling for the beauties of nature which has rarely been equalled in any style of ornament. It would be beyond the scope of this volume to give a more extensive set of examples of these decorations than those on Plate II. and at Fig. 29 and more especially as the ornament applied to costume was, in the main, of a geometric nature : but it will be of the utmost interest to the student of Aegean dress to follow up the references given as to the books in which fine examples are illustrated.* We do not possess in the British Museum anything like a representative Minoan ornament exhibit, it being now the custom for valuable archaeological discoveries to be preserved in the museums of the countries where they are found and therefore the originals are chiefly at Candia Museum in Crete. For this reason we are obliged to get our knowledge from books and photographs. In the beautiful naturalistic ornament which existed when the style was at its best, the sea has suggested some of the finest motifs to the Minoan designers. One splendid example has for its subject swimming fish against a background of fishermen's nets and sea spray ; there are beautiful treatments of swaying seaweed and of shells ; even that fearsome denizen of the sea—the octopus— is made into a wonderful piece of decoration with his terrible head and far-stretching tentacles. On the painted walls we find friezes also inspired by the warrior's armour and weapons. The frieze border of the " double axe-heads," that sacred symbol in the Minoan religion, and that of the " dappled bull's-hide shields " are fine examples (see Figs. 29c and 30).

* See, for example, *The Palace of Minos at Knossos* by Sir Arthur Evans.

It is difficult to describe, in words, the beauty of the Minoan treatment of floral ornament as seen especially in the frescoes of the end of the Middle and commencement of the Late Minoan Periods. Just as the exquisite designs of swaying seaweed and marine creatures delight the eye in Minoan pottery designs, so in the frescoes we see the fields of spring and summer flowers treated with a most tender and delicate appreciation of nature. Even tree-growths such as the olive are designed to show the wind swaying in their branches as the sea does amid the seaweeds. The young priest-king at Fig. 12 walks through a field of flowers over which hover lovely butterflies. While the flowers in the priest-king's field are chiefly irises, the white Easter Lily, the saffron-flower or crocus, the wild rose and other blooms too numerous to mention riot over these frescoed walls ; whilst among trees the olive is perhaps the favourite. Birds and animals are also depicted with marvellous skill, and one example of the somewhat rare use of naturalistic ornament in dress decoration is that of a design with flying swallows seen upon a lady's skirt.

Details of Ornament on Plate II.*

These examples are all of the more formal or severe type of Aegean ornament, and some show signs of Egyptian influences, a natural outcome of the intercourse between near-by countries.

Fig. *a* is from Tiryns, 1400 B.C.–1200 B.C. and will be recognized as ornament from the flounces of the priestess, Fig. 22. The method of colour arrangement in the white, red, orange, blue band, 1, 2, 3, 4, 1, 2, 3, 4, is identical with the method of the Egyptians, who used a similar border design on their mummy cases.

* See inside front cover for color version.

Fig. *b* is from Pseira in Crete and of the Late Minoan Period. It is from a fresco or wall-painting showing a woman's costume. The drawing here was made from a photograph, and the colour scheme has been taken from another contemporary example to show that the use of green was not unknown, though the red, yellow and blue scheme was more popular.

Fig. *c* is from the flounce of a lady's skirt and is also from Crete ; dating is Late Minoan Period. The Cretan fondness for the spiral as an element in decorative design will be noticed in this and many other examples.

Fig. *d* is from the painted sarcophagus at Hagia Triada and is used as a border to the figure-subject showing at Figs. 13 and 14.

Fig. *e* is from a piece of Cretan pottery of Mid-Minoan Period. It slightly resembles some of the ornaments on Greek pottery of the fifth and fourth century B.C.

Fig. *f* is from Tiryns, dating 1400 B.C.–1200 B.C., and is used to border the wall-painting from which the figure of the priestess at Fig. 22 is taken. The same pattern in simpler form is seen on the bodice of the priestess.

Fig. *g* is also from a wall-painting at Tiryns, of the same date as Fig. *f* and is evidently copied from an Egyptian pattern by the Mycenaean designer, who has, however, given it quite an original character in his treatment of the detail and in his colour scheme.

All the examples of Aegean ornament at Fig. 29 are copied from exhibits shown in the British Museum Greek pottery galleries.

Fig. 29*a* is a votive dress in pottery from the same collection as the Snake Goddess at Fig. 7, and is apparently a back view. The seams of the bodice are differently planned from

Fig. 29.

those shown at Figs. 7a, b and c. There is again a double
rolled padded girdle round the waist, the apron effects seem
to be at each side instead of back and front, but this may
be owing to the rather imperfect notions of primitive drawing
and because the artist wished to give more room to display
his beautiful decoration of flowers. This is an example of
the naturalistic style in Minoan decoration. It shows a
clump of the sacred saffron-flower treated after the manner
of Ancient Egyptian lotus or papyrus designs. A wind-
blown border of the same flower is below.

Fig. 29b is from Rhodes and is dated 1400 B.C.–1250 B.C.
and slightly naturalistic in style.

Figs. 29d, 29e, 29h and 29i are from Greece and dated
1600 B.C.–1400 B.C. ; Fig. 29c shows the " double axe-head "
pattern already mentioned.

Fig. 29f is a portion of the repeating pattern on the
bodice of Figs. 7a, b and c, drawn out to a larger scale. It
is an example of the favourite spiral motif.

Figs. 29g and 29k are from painted vases.

Fig. 29j is from a Minoan votive pottery girdle. The
pattern is drawn on one of the double padded roll girdles
similar to that on Fig. 29a, and the line between the two
rolls is indicated in the drawing.

Fig. 30 shows a portion of one of the characteristic figure-
of-eight Aegean shield borders. The treatment of the
dappled bull's hide covering the shield is wonderfully decorative. In the frieze from which this is taken the dappling on
the shields is grey, red and black, alternately repeating on
the white groundwork of each shield. The whole formed a
frieze on the palace wall.

No examples of Minoan jewellery are illustrated in this
volume, though some very beautiful specimens have come

PLATE II.—CRETAN ORNAMENT.

(See inside front cover for color version.)

to light, as, for instance, the delicate floral rosette designs for the
heads of golden pins and also
beads from necklaces. At the
same time it must be said that in
the realm of jewellery the discoveries in Minoan Crete, up to
the present, are not of the rich and
profuse magnificence which has
characterized the treasures yielded
up by graves of Ancient Egypt
and Mesopotamia. On the other
hand, in Southern Greece, since
the discoveries by Schliemann and
afterwards by others; it has been
made clear that this mainland
offshoot of Aegean civilization

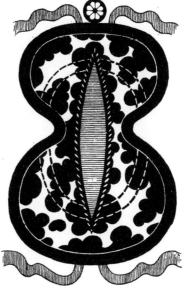

Fig. 30.

had in its rulers a race of kings who possessed great
treasures in the shape of golden ornaments. Figs. 31*a*,
b, *c* and *d* were discovered by Schliemann in the " Third
Shaft Grave " at Mycenae. Fig. 31*a* is a golden diadem ; it
would be worn covering the forehead and kept in position
by an inserted cord or ribbon tied at the back of the head.
Diadems precisely similar in shape are seen on statuettes and
seals found at Ur in Mesopotamia. For example, *see* Fig. 31*e*
which is from a seal-impression dating *c.* 2000 B.C. Here it
is interesting to note (*see* also Chapter II.) we have a mode
of dressing the hair common to both men and women in the
earlier ages of Greek (Hellenic) costume. Figs. 31*b* and *c*
are circular golden ornaments, thought to be used as a dress
decoration by sewing on as a diaper over the surface of the
material (*see* perhaps after the manner indicated at Figs.

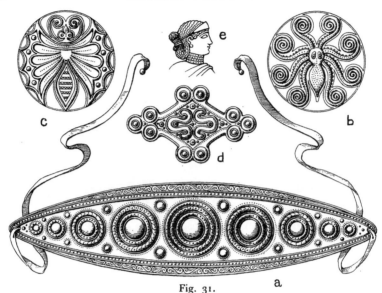

Fig. 31.

7*d* and 25). The subject of Fig. 31*b* is a representation of the octopus, which, as has been said (p. 26), was a favourite motif of the artists who decorated Minoan pottery. Fig. 31*c*, a butterfly, also figures frequently in Minoan art (Fig. 12. The priest-king is described on p. 27 as walking in a flowery meadow over which butterflies hover). The butterfly was among the Aegeans, as afterwards among the Greeks, a religious symbol. Fig. 31*d* is called by Schliemann a button. This golden button, like the diadem, is decorated with geometric ornament chiefly circular in its detail.

With the foregoing examples of Minoan and Mycenaean costume and ornament we must take leave of that " Golden Age " of a civilization to which classical Hellas looked back and to which Homer referred as that " old time of peace before the Achaeans* came."

* It was not, in fact, the semi-civilized Achaeans, but the invading Dorians who followed them to whom the destruction of Aegean civilization was due.

CHAPTER II

ANCIENT GREEK COSTUME

WITH the downfall of Aegean civilization, *c.* 1100 B.C., comes that obscure " Dark Age " about which we have so little information. Indeed the Homeric Poems, which are said to have been written between the ninth and eighth centuries B.C., reflecting as they do the life of their time, are almost the sole source of our knowledge. In the realm of costume, for example, we read of the " many-brooched peplos " worn by Homer's Achaean ladies, showing that he did not visualize the tight bodice and flounced petticoat of the Minoan and Mycenaean Periods, but rather those simple rectangular pieces of woven stuff upon which much of later Greek costume was based. It should be remembered that, like all the ancients, Homer was unaware of the past except so far as oral tradition informed him ; and like those tapestry designers of the sixteenth and seventeenth centuries A.D. in Western Europe, who have represented Helen of Troy and her lover, Paris, dressed in ruffs and stiff padded garments, Homer saw his heroes and heroines clad in the costume of his day, though they were the people of an age some 250 years previous to his own and may have worn Aegean dress. When exactly the flounced skirt and tight bodice of the Aegean women and the kilt, aprons or short drawers of the men disappeared we cannot tell.

That " Dark Age " pottery, the so-called " Dipylon Ware "

Fig. 32.

c. 800 B.C., discovered at Athens and elsewhere, shows wasp-waisted men and women whose silhouette is similar to that of the frescoes of Knossos and Mycenae; also Archaic Greek statues of the seventh to sixth century B.C., now in the Louvre, exhibit a woman in tight corset bodice and a man also with wasp waist and Minoan metal belt. These point to a survival in some respects of Aegean costume; on the other hand in that magnificent specimen of early Greek pottery, the François Vase *c.* 650 B.C. (*see* Fig. 32) the costume of both men and women is entirely Greek in character. It must also be remembered when considering the Aegean styles as described in Chapter I. that what is called Mainland dress existed both in Crete and at Mycenae on the Greek mainland at the same time as the flounced skirts and double-aprons (*see* Figs. 14 and 27 on the one hand, and Figs. 22 and 23 on the other). Probably the exotic elaborations of certain types of Aegean costume were merely a passing fancy which in that remote period lasted very much longer than would a similar craze in the modern world, where change *must* come perforce if the dress designer and manufacturer are to remain solvent. Again, it is curious to reflect in connection with the so-called " peasant costume " of women in many European countries where the corset bodice and full petticoat suggest a resemblance to the Aegean ladies, that here there is hint of a survival which may have lingered on in some remote district to undergo a resurrection in the course of the centuries. When, at some future date, the Greek mainland and the opposite coast of Asia have been excavated by archaeologists to the same extent as has

been done in Crete, Egypt and Mesopotamia our ignorance
of this " Dark Age " of transition may be dispelled. Greek
art, as a whole, has been divided into periods by various
authorities. One arrangement of dating is as follows :

(1) The Archaic Period, 600 B.C–480 B.C. The costumes
    of this period correspond more closely than any
    other to those described in Homer.

(2) What is sometimes called the Fine Period of the
    fifth century, 480 B.C.–400 B.C. This includes
    the Age of Pericles.

(3) The fourth century, which includes the Alexandrian
    Era, 400 B.C.–320 B.C.

(4) The Hellenistic Age, 320 B.C.–100 B.C. The fall of
    Greek independence occurred in 146 B.C. and this
    led to the Graeco-Roman Period.

Before examining the representative types of true Greek
costume it is of interest to record a resemblance,
possibly only superficial, to the characteristic flap or

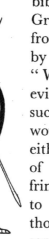

bib which was such a feature of the
Greek Doric style of dress. Fig. 33 is
from a late Mycenaean vase discovered
by Schliemann which is known as the
"Warrior Vase." This soldier's dress is
evidently of very thick and stiff material,
such as leather or padded and stiffened
woven stuff, the fringe at the bottom being
either strips of cut leather or the threads
of the warp formed into a tasselled
fringe. The leggings are not dissimilar
to those worn by Figs. 15 and 26
though Fig. 33 has apparently some
sort of boot in addition to his leggings.

Fig. 33.

The quaintly shaped helmet with its horns and horse-hair crest is distinctive as is also the shield which he carries.

To describe Greek costume from the purely chronological aspect would not give, by any means, the clearest view of the style, characterized as it is by the persistence of certain types. In contrast to modern and even to mediaeval fashions, in which the year or the century shows a definite style pertaining to that time and no other, there is little in Greek costume which corresponds. Though the materials and decorations show change and development, the construction remains simple and almost unchanged from the Archaic Period to the Hellenistic Age. It seems best, therefore, that we should study the whole subject from a stylistic and structural standpoint in the first place, not forgetting, of course, that *in a minor degree* there were certain changes through the centuries, more especially in those types where Asiatic influences were at work.

The sources from which we get our information are not, as is well known, from actual costumes. Only a very few fragments of actual Greek garments have been preserved to us (*see* Plate III.). For our notions of style and shape we are therefore dependent on the representative arts and on references in literature. Many of the illustrations in this chapter are taken from vase-paintings, as the Greek artists who specialized in this form of decoration are, for the most part, extremely accurate in their delineations of costume. The Archaic artist, however, had not always the power of expression needed, and the artists of the two latest ages exhibit a certain flamboyance in their drawing at the expense of accuracy. On the other hand, the painters of the Fine Period display both skill in delineation and a restrained correctness of drawing which makes their work invaluable to the student of costume. Again Greek sculpture supplies us with useful data for costume, but here perhaps it is the Archaic Period which gives the most accurate view. The sculpture of the Fine Period, unequalled for its representation of the human figure, shows a certain freedom in its treatment of drapery which, at times, loses the exactness necessary when representing costume so that its type can be accurately classified from the structural aspect.

We find that, in general, the whole style of Greek costume depends on the hang or set of the materials as drapery, and we may contrast these effects with those fitted and semifitted garments which were worn by nations such as the Cretans (see Chap. I., present volume), the Persians (see Vol. I., *Ancient Egyptian, Mesopotamian and Persian Costume*),* the Scythians, Phrygians (see Figs. 77 and 79) and others, all of which fitted garments suggest an origin, not in woven materials, but in the dressed skins of animals, and in a few cases, not here cited, possibly knitted fabrics. The Greek costumes may be likened more to those of ancient Egypt and Mesopotamia (see Vol. I.), where draping rather than fitting was the mode.

The materials used in Greek costume varied with the centuries. As is natural, the more ancient examples show a thicker weave and also the primitive love for lavish decoration, whilst the later and more highly developed art displays a restraint and reticence in the decoration, and the thinner, more supple fabrics, show to great advantage the figure of the wearer.

The most used material in Greek costume was wool of both coarse and fine weave, and rather loose in texture, so that it draped well. Next to wool, linen was of most frequent wear, which, like the woollen stuffs, varied in weave from

* The first edition was entitled *Ancient Egyptian, Assyrian and Persian Costume.* It is available from Dover Publications (0-486-42562-2).

coarse to very fine transparent stuff. Silk was not unknown to the Greeks, but it was rare. Most of the silk was manu-factured in the island of Cos, but most probably the raw material came from Asia. Those specimens of Greek materials which remain to us were found at Kertch in the Crimea (*see* Plate III.), and belong to the fifth or fourth century B.C. One of these fragments is of silk, and the ornamentation of the several fragments shows that various methods of decoration were known to the Greeks. We have, for example, (*a*) simple geometric designs woven into the material ; (*b*) rather more elaborate tapestry weaving, such as we see in Graeco-Roman fragments from Egypt ; (*c*) the well-known " honeysuckle," " anthemion " or " palmette " pattern, elaborately embroidered ; and lastly, (*d*) one specimen is decorated with painted ornament (*see* again Plate III.).

The Doric and Ionic Styles

These names have been given to the two outstanding types of Greek dress, but, distinct as they are, an infinite number of dresses existed which partook of the characteristics of both styles. The merging of the styles is perhaps more evident in the later examples, as indeed it is natural to expect. Herodotus tells us that " the real national Greek dress was the Doric whereas the Ionic was adopted by the Greeks of Asia from that of their neighbours, the Carians." The essentially Greek Doric was at first distinct from the more Asiatic Ionic, but each eventually losing its separate identity, became merged in one great and varied Greek style. While the Doric and Ionic types dominated Greek costumes, we are constantly presented, in the vase-paintings, with representations of various foreign dresses, such as those from Phrygia, already mentioned, and the nearer coasts of Asia Minor. There is a whole group of costumes with rather tight, short tunics of distinctive appearance, which are, possibly, Asiatic in origin. The foreign dresses, as worn by women, would often be the costume of slaves from abroad ; eventually in the later ages of Greek dress they became a strong influence in the wear of all classes. On the latest period of Greek dress and throughout the Roman Era both Asiatic and Egyptian influences were at work in Greece and Italy, and there is little doubt the changes which thereby ensued helped to produce what we know as Byzantine costume, the latest style described in this volume. While these changes took place in the costume of the chief centres of civilization, Byzantium and Rome, Greek dress survived, no doubt, in more remote countries, which had been long under Greek and Roman domination. An instance of this is shown in the costume of the Kabyle women of North Africa, who still wear Greek Doric costumes in the present day.

THE DORIC DRESS AS WORN BY GREEK WOMEN

This garment, called by the Greeks the Doric chiton (*chiton*=dress), is perhaps the most characteristic part of all Greek costume, and was the most ancient type of their women's dress. We learn from Herodotus that up to the beginning of the sixth century B.C. it was in universal wear among Grecian women, and he tells, to account for the introduction of the second or Ionic type of chiton (dress), the following story : " After a disastrous military expedition by the Athenian army, where all the defeated forces were

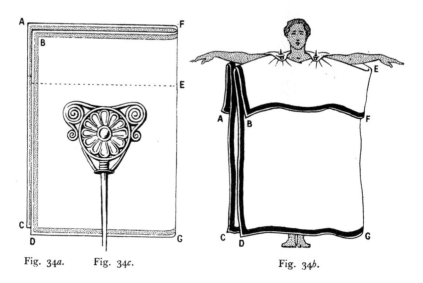

Fig. 34a.   Fig. 34c.   Fig. 34b.

put to death with the exception of one man, who, escaping, returned to tell the disconsolate women of Athens the fate of their men, the women then took the huge pins (*see* Fig. 32), with which their Doric chitons were fastened on the shoulders, and with them stabbed this man to death in their rage and contempt. The Athenians thought this piece of feminine ferocity even worse than the fate of their troops, and to punish the women decreed that hereafter they should wear the Ionic dress, which does not require pins.'' This story points out the fact that, for some reason, in the beginning of the sixth century, Ionic dress began to be worn in Athens and possibly other parts of Greece.

The Doric chiton in its most simple and characteristic form was an oblong of woollen cloth measuring about twice the width of the wearer from elbow to elbow when the arms were outstretched, and about eighteen inches more than her height from shoulder to ground. The stuff was folded

Fig. 35.

across at the height of the shoulders, allowing the superfluous eighteen inches to fall down outside in a flap all along the top edge. This folded overpiece is the chief and unique feature of the dress, the second feature being that it was fastened, back to front, on each shoulder with large pins. We now come to the variations of the style. The most simple and characteristic type was that illustrated at Fig. 35, and in Sparta, famed for preserving the primitive severity of early Greek customs, it was so worn. The dimensions depended on the height of the wearer, as suggested above. Figs. 34a and 34b on p. 40 will explain the method of adjustment. The border shown in these diagrams would be woven into the garment, which was made the correct size on the loom, not cut out in any way. This example is worn without a girdle, and, as will be seen, leaves one side of the figure quite nude, as was approved by the Spartans, who cultivated hardness of body, and later, in a more luxurious age, it served for display. In diagram 34a the line of folding is shown as a dotted line. In 34b the garment has been pinned on each shoulder, back over front, and it is shown spread out as if the model were lying on her back on the floor. Fig. 34c is the head of a gold pin found at Troy. Fig. 35 (dating fifth century B.C.) shows the garment in wear ; in this case it is pinned on back over front, hence the pins do not show.

The examples 36a and 37a show two types of early or archaic Doric dress. Fig. 36a is dated sixth century B.C., and is from a representation of the goddess Artemis (her bow and quiver not being shown in this illustration). It is cut in a similar manner to Fig. 35, p. 41, but differs in three respects : first, it is very much tighter ; and second, it is sewn together all the way up instead of being left open like Fig. 35 ; third, it is girded. Fig. 36b is a diagram making the

Fig. 36a.

Fig. 38.

Fig. 37a.

Fig. 36b.

Fig. 39.

Fig. 37b.

Fig. 40a.

cut of Fig. 36a more clear. It has been necessary, however, to draw this diagram with a rather looser dress than 36a, for the sake of clearer explanation and also because 36a was probably not really quite so tight as it seems to be in the primitive vase-painting of the sixth century B.C. To ensure that the skirt portion of these two chitons 36b and 37b will hang with an even line, the garment must be held out horizontally along the top edge by the wearer while another person ties the girdle in each case. The girdles are shown at *i, j, k, l*. Behind each diagram of the garment in wear, at *A, B, C, D* and *E, F, G, H*, each garment is also shown spread out flat at *a, b, c, d* and *e, f, g, h*. The fold-over in the flat plans is indicated as a dotted line. In Fig. 36b the seam, which is at one side only, is indicated by dots. Fig. 37a is dated end of the sixth century B.C. This dress differs from 36a in being a little wider and longer, and it also has the flap or over-fold left open at both sides instead of closed as in 36a. There would most probably have been a seam on both sides of 37a, and this is indicated in the diagram 37b. The musician (Fig. 38) is also of the sixth century B.C., and should be compared with two Etruscan figures given later in this volume; it is set down here to show the variety in sixth century B.C. fashions. Fig. 39 is an Archaic Greek

Fig. 40b.

silver pin dedicated to the goddess Hera. It was found in Argolis, and is now in the British Museum. It is, of course, drawn to a very large scale compared to the costumes.

Figs. 40a and 41 (from vase-paintings in the British Museum, of the fifth century B.C.) show two other ways of adjusting the Doric chiton. Fig. 40a shows a garment with a much longer over-fold than Fig. 35, p. 41, and it is girded, but not as in Figs. 36a and 37a, *under* the over-fold. This type has the girdle *on the top* of the fold and is often called the Peplos of Athena ; the celebrated statue of Athena Parthenos being thus draped. Fig. 40b, another representation of the goddess Athena, is taken from the well-known memorial relief ("Stele") entitled "The Mourning Athena"; it is of the fifth century B.C., and from the collection at the Museum of the Acropolis, Athens. Here we see a similar draping of the Doric chiton or peplos to that at Fig. 40a, but, in addition, the goddess is wearing her characteristic Corinthian helmet, pushed back from the face, and it is of interest to compare the head here with that of the figure of Britannia on an English penny, the design of the head of the latter figure having that of the Greek goddess as its inspiration. The word "peplos" here means precisely the same as "chiton." The artist who drew Fig. 40a has exaggerated the zigzag effect of

Fig. 41.

the folds down the open side of this garment. The cascade or zigzag effect in folds was immensely admired by the Greek artists, who always emphasized and generally exaggerated it in their representations. Fig. 41 is of similar make to the Archaic Greek dress, Fig. 36a, p. 43, but the over-fold is very much longer and the girdle is on the top of the fold, not below it. The sewing of the one seam is very evident, and in some cases we find it still more emphasized with rich decoration. The similarity between Fig. 32 from the François Vase and Fig. 36a is easily discerned.

The Doric style in *women's* dress has been given the foremost place because as in the case of Aegean costume of *men* often appeared nude or almost nude and when clothed their dress was simple and scanty except perhaps when the person was elderly or of great social importance. The Doric chiton of the Greek man was short and not ample. Usually it was fastened on both shoulders, but it passed under the right arm and was fastened on the left shoulder only, when worn by workmen—Fig. 42 from a bronze statue of Hephaestus in the British Museum shows the man's Doric dress as worn by a Greek workman. The cap and high boots are characteristic and were worn by workmen and travellers.

Fig. 42.

THE IONIC DRESS AS WORN
BY GREEK WOMEN

The style of dress known as "Ionic," to which reference has already been made on p. 38, is said to have been introduced into Greece from Caria (on the coast of Asia Minor). It was of thin linen and often transparent, and had no over-fold such as we find in the Doric. The drawing of the Ionic tunic (*chiton*), Fig. 43c on p. 49, is from a vase-painting of the fifth century B.C. (the figure appears distorted because of the curve of the vase). The woman is in the act of tying her girdle. On p. 48 the diagrams, Figs. 43a and 43b, A, B, C, D and a, b, c, d, will give a more exact idea of the cut and method of wear. In this, the most characteristically Ionic type, the armholes are in the *top* edge of the garment, in line with the neck hole, and it is to this fact the beauty of the under-arm draperies of Greek Ionic dresses is due. At times, however, the armholes were slit in the sides, not the top, and Fig. 44a, W, X, Y, Z, corresponding to A, B, C, D in 43a, draws attention to this fact. Fig. 44a is that of a youthful Greek warrior of the end of the fifth century B.C. His high-laced boots (*endromides*) are characteristic.

Fig. 44b is an example of the Ionic chiton shortened by draping and so made suitable for wear by women engaged in athletic pursuits. It is a drawing from the well-known " Artemis of Versailles " now in the Louvre. (Gardner

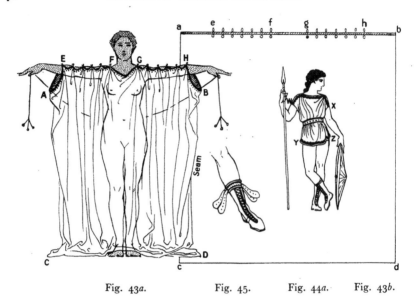

Fig. 43a.   Fig. 45.   Fig. 44a.   Fig. 43b.

assigns the date of this figure to the Hellenistic Age.)   Here
we have the chiton folded in two, but unevenly. As will
be seen, the shorter part barely reaches to the hips while the
longer comes down to the knees. The wide girdle shown
on Fig. 44b is frequently seen on representations of Artemis
(the " Artemis succincta "—so called, as referring to this
girdle).

Fig. 44c.   The well-known " Wounded Amazon " after
Polycleitus—a Roman copy from a Greek fifth-century B.C.
original, and now in the Capitoline Museum, Rome, shows
another method of shortening the chiton which, in this case,
would not at full length extend much below the knee.   Here
the shortening is effected by the double girdle, so frequently
used on both Doric and Ionic costumes of walking length
(see Figs. 50 and 60).   The chiton here is fastened on one
shoulder only (in this case the right shoulder) as is frequently

Fig. 43c.

seen in Greek representations of Amazons. These legendary woman warriors are also represented with a similar chiton fastened on both shoulders and having a narrow girdle crossed over the breast, which girdle is shown at Fig. 59a. Other representations of Amazons in Greek costume show a full-length chiton shortened by the double girdle so that it is only knee-length and hence has an immensely large hanging fold (or *kolpos*) in place of the comparatively small one shown at Fig. 44c. It should also be said that Amazons in Greek dress often wear the short cloak (*chlamys*) in addition to the tunic (*chiton*). Very frequently also the Amazons are represented in Phrygian costume and at Fig. 77, there is an example of this type of dress. Fig. 45, a very gallant-looking example of the

Fig. 44c.

same type of boot, is from the figure of an Amazon. The Greeks often represented Amazons dressed in a similar manner to Fig. 44a.

Ionic dress is generally fastened along the top edge by a series of small brooches or buttons, as shown in Figs. 43a, 43b and 43c. Fig. 46a on p. 52, which is from a vase-painting of the sixth century B.C., may be said to be a variety of the Ionic. It is fastened along the top with buttons or clasps, but, on the other hand, the armholes are not in the top edge. On the contrary, it is really the well-known T-shaped tunic common to almost all the nations of antiquity ; the small clasps or buttons being the only truly Greek feature ; the

Fig. 44*b*.

cutting out is shown in Fig. 46b. Fig. 48, also of the sixth century B.C., is exactly the same type of dress except that the sleeves are tighter and somewhat longer than those of Fig. 46, and there are no clasps. The garment is sewn down the line where the clasps should come. Fig. 47a, which dates end of the sixth century B.C., wears an Ionic chiton really identical in shape with that of the youthful warrior, Fig. 44a, p. 48, except that it is very much longer

Fig. 46b.

Fig. 46a.

Fig. 47b.

Fig. 47a.

Fig. 48.

and wider. The plan is shown at Fig. 47b, where the slits for arms and neck are shown; again in this dress there are no clasps, it is sewn up. The different varieties of hairdressing through the centuries can be observed throughout this volume.

The illustrations on the next page will draw attention to the very considerable varieties in style which were worn

Fig. 49.   Fig. 50.   Fig. 51.

by the Greek woman at any one time during the centuries.
Figs. 49, 50 and 51 are of the middle of the fifth century,
the .Fine Period of Greek art. Fig. 49, the musician, is
wearing an Ionic chiton, the armholes being in the top edge
as in Fig. 43*a*. There are, however, no clasps on this dress ;
it is sewn, as we find in many types of Ionic. The extreme
width of this dress would tend to let it slip off the shoulders,
so that crossed cords are worn to prevent this (*see* illustration).
The dress is quite thirty inches longer than the figure and
hangs in an immense pouch (Gk. *kolpos*) over the concealed
girdle. Fig. 50 is wearing a style which seems to be a mixture
of Doric with Ionic. The over-fold has a slit at the side to
allow of an armhole. The dress is immensely long and girded
twice, the lower girdle being concealed. Fig. 51 is a pure
Doric chiton of the closed type.

Fig. 52.   Fig. 53.   Fig. 54.

The three figures given on this page show further variations from the true Doric and Ionic types of Greek costume.
Fig. 52, which is from a vase-painting of the end of the sixth
century B.C., is wearing an Ionic chiton of thin material,
which is only visible on one arm and about the shoulders.
Over this she has a species of Doric chiton of thicker stuff
which she is about to fasten on one shoulder. The over-fold
is open at both sides, and she has an immense pouch or
kolpos hanging over a concealed girdle. Her hair is tied
up at the end in a little bag and then bound with cords
in the Archaic fashion. Fig. 53, which is that of the god
Seilenos in characteristic dress, is also of the end of the sixth
century B.C. He is wearing the true type of Ionic chiton,
similar to that shown on p. 48; but attached to the neck,
both back and front, is a small over-fold or bib which gives
the garment a Doric detail. Over his transparent chiton
he has an embroidered tunic or corselet of stiff linen, which

Fig. 55.   Fig. 56.   Fig. 57.

fits tightly and would be fastened at one side. The bib or over-fold hangs down and partly hides this corselet. Fig. 54, which is of the fifth century B.C., wears a transparent Ionic chiton underneath, and over it a species of Doric which has, however, slits at the sides for armholes, and the neck-opening is hidden by a decorated collar which would fasten at the back. If this collar were part of the dress, which it does not appear to be, it would be fastened with a small button and loop on one shoulder, leaving a slit wide enough to admit of the garment being pulled over the head.

The three figures on this page show unusual costumes, and Figs. 56 and 57 are distinctly foreign importations. Fig. 55, which belongs to the fifth century B.C., is wearing rather a tight Ionic chiton underneath, and over it a tunic very similar in shape to that worn by the youthful warrior, Fig. 44a,

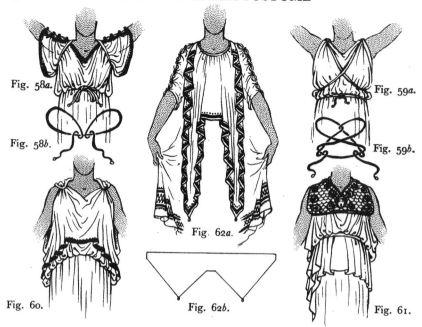

Fig. 58a.

Fig. 58b.

Fig. 59a.

Fig. 59b.

Fig. 62a.

Fig. 60.

Fig. 62b.

Fig. 61.

on p. 48. This tunic is therefore Ionic in type, but is of thick material. The decoration is curiously similar in shape to that found on Egypto-Roman tunics of the sixth century A.D. Fig. 56, which is dated end of the fifth century B.C., is that of an Asiatic slave. The richly decorated shoulder part is characteristically Asiatic or Egyptian and foreshadows Byzantine costume many hundreds of years later. Fig. 57, which is dated fifth century B.C., has a most unusual type of tunic worn over a thinner under-dress. The decoration is somewhat similar to that on Fig. 55, and both these dresses seem to have an affinity to the Etruscan style (*see* next chapter); but Fig. 57, who is an attendant behind the throne of Midas (King of Phrygia, 700 B.C.), is most probably in a species of Phrygian dress.

The diagrams Figs. 58a and b and 59a and b, above, draw

attention to the method of tying crossed cords round the arms or over the breast and back when wearing the Ionic chiton. Fig. 58a, in which a cord about two yards long is looped over each armpit in front (*see* diagram) and then tied in the middle of the back between the shoulder-blades, shows the method employed to give freedom to the arms and to keep on a very wide chiton. This method of tying is seen on the Greek charioteers who, at one period, wore long Ionic tunics. The drawing Fig. 58a shows this method of tying on a woman, and is from the chiton of Thalia, Muse of Comedy, in the British Museum Galleries. Fig. 58b is a drawing of the cord as it is twisted just before tying in a knot. Figs. 59a and b show another method of arranging the cord. This method appears nearly always on the dresses of women ; it is rarely found on men, and then only in the very late periods. It tends to keep the garment trim over the body, and we find Fig. 59a at times on the Amazons, to allow of freedom of movement in battle. The cord for this method is about $3\frac{1}{2}$ yards long and is drawn out in diagram at Fig. 59b. It is adjusted by placing the middle of the cord at centre-back of waist, then bringing round each end of the cord under the arms, crossing in centre-breast and throwing upwards over each shoulder to the back. The cords are then drawn down behind each shoulder and twisted round as at 59b before being brought round and tied in front of waist. This method, as shown in wear on Fig. 59a, is over a tight Ionic chiton which has slits at the sides for armholes. It will be seen the cord forms a girdle as well as a crossing over. There is a third method in which the cords are crossed in front as in Fig. 59a, but are tied behind as in 58a and b, and therefore do not come down as low as the girdle, which is a separate affair both in this style and in the 58a and b method.

Fig. 58c.

Fig. 60, p. 56, is from a Doric dress (*peplos*) of the fifth century B.C., and shows the very decorative kolpos or baggy fold under the over-flap. This dress is cut fairly wide, otherwise the graceful droop of the kolpos and over-fold at each side would be less pronounced. The " Caryatid of the Erechtheum," now in the British Museum, wears a dress of this type. Fig. 61 shows the arrangement known as the " Peplos of Athena," and over it her " aegis " (as it is sculptured on the small copy of the statue of Athena Parthenos, fifth century B.C.), with its borders of serpents, scale-patterned background and Medusa's head. Fig. 62a shows a rather elaborately beautiful treatment of the Ionic chiton with a bib or fold attached by gathering into a band at the neck ; Fig. 62b (which is $\frac{1}{4}$ scale of 62a) shows the cutting out of the bib. This costume is of a late type, and would not be worn until the Alexandrian or the Hellenistic Period.

Fig. 62c is a drawing from Hope's *Costume of the Ancients* showing the dress in wear as the Greek artist saw it. Fig. 58c is a drawing of the " Charioteer of Delphi," a bronze life-size statue of *c.* 474 B.C., now in the museum at Delphi. In the original statue the left arm is missing and would probably have been held in the same position as is the right while driving. It is here drawn

Fig. 62c.

hanging down in order to display the draping of the chiton as explained in the diagrams 58a and b.

Fig. 63 shows the goddess Athena in Ionic dress, the draping of which can be well understood by comparing it with the diagrams at Figs. 64a and b,* and also with the costume shown at Fig. 65. This drawing is taken from a vase-painting adorning an Attic cup which dates c. 480 B.C. The original is in the Vatican. Over her Ionic chiton and himation the goddess wears the aegis in its transitional form (Fig. 61, p. 56, showing its latest conventionalized shape). The earliest representations of this combined shield and breast-plate show it as a goat-skin tied round the neck by the two forelegs; the remainder of the skin hanging down over

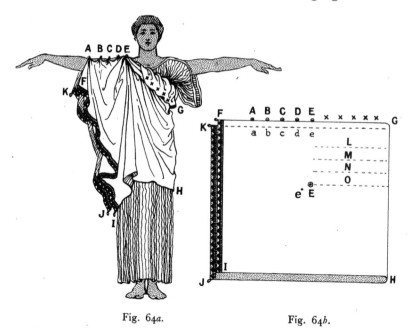

Fig. 64a.   Fig. 64b.

* It will be seen, however, that while Figs. 63 and 65 have the drapery slung under the right armpit, in Figs. 64c and d it is under the left.

Fig. 63.

the left arm and capable of being raised to protect the body
as a shield.   Later the origin of the aegis was forgotten, and
it is shown as if covered with metal scales as at Fig. 61.   In
the latest types as at Fig. 61, it is merely a protection for the
breast and back.   The Medusa's head is prominent, as is also
the fringe of serpents on Fig. 63.   A very full account of the
aegis is given in Smith's Classical Dictionary.   The magnificent golden helmet of Fig. 63 is surmounted by a ridge and
crest of horse-hair, and the head-piece is adorned with a
fabulous animal on either side.   Few public libraries are
without classical dictionaries and other works in which the
masterpieces of Greek sculpture are illustrated.   It will
therefore be of interest to the student of costume to extend
his knowledge by comparing the types illustrated in the
present volume with those easily accessible works to which
reference has been made.

Women's Outdoor Dress

There is an excellent example of this dress in wear,
on a bronze statuette of the fifth century B.C. now in the
British Museum from which the drawing 64c has been taken.
In the original the right hand is damaged and is here re-
stored.   The back view of the statuette shows, as part of the
elaborate coiffure, a solid cascade of waved hair hanging
almost to the waist ; this, in addition to the six massive
ringlets falling over the shoulders in front and the two great
swathes of hair wound round the head.   The eyes of this
beautiful little figure are of diamonds, inset.   Fig. 64d is from
a vase-painting and again shows the same costume.   This
drawing is here given in order to settle a controversial point
regarding the dress of these figures which has been a subject

Fig. 64c.   Fig. 64d.

of discussion among archaeologists. The earlier writers, when describing the garments as seen in Figs. 64c and d, and having regard to the fact that the upper part of the chiton—that which covers the body is often represented as of crinkled material and the lower part which covers the legs is indicated by plain folds—considered that this was not one simple Ionic tunic but two separate garments. This view was seemingly upheld by the fact that those well-known Archaic statues of maidens (Korai) discovered at Athens are painted

Fig. 65.   Fig. 66.   Fig. 67b.

in colours, and here again the portion of the chiton which
covers the body is often different in tint from that covering
the lower limbs.   Among the later authorities, however,
there is a general agreement that the garment in dispute
is really one simple tunic, which view the representation of
it on Fig. 64d goes to prove, for here we see that much of the
upper part is left plain without any indication of the crinkled
lines ; also a comparison with Figs. 65 and 66 will show that
these two later figures form a natural sequence to the
preceding style.

When in Doric dress, the Grecian women seldom added
an outdoor garment, as the thick woollen material of their
chiton was sufficient, save in really cold weather, and the over-
fold at the back could be lifted up over the head if need be.
At times a small oblong head-veil was worn and also a cloak,

but it is for the thinner Ionic chiton that the need of an
outdoor wrap is obvious. This cloak (Gk. *himation*, worn
by both sexes) or wrap of fairly thick woollen material which
varied in size was rectangular in shape and was adjusted in
many modes through the centuries, the earliest and simplest
being that similar to the shoulder-wrap worn by an early
sixth century B.C. statue from Attica (original now in Berlin
Museum) shown at Fig. 67a and which represents a priestess
or goddess. Her wrap is folded and worn over an Ionic
chiton of apparently rather thick woollen material. She
holds in her hand a pomegranate. Another figure showing
an equally simple method of wear is shown on the man's
costume, Fig. 69a. At the end of the Archaic Period we find
the himation on women, and at times on men, arranged in
quite an elaborate manner, with almost as
much searching after effect as is seen in the
studied elegancies of the Roman toga. This
Archaic Greek himation was an intricate affair,
and it is only by studying the gradual change
of mode as seen in Figs, 64a, 65, 66, that we
can understand it. The diagram 64a, p. 60,
shows the Archaic women's himation as worn,
and 64b shows it folded in two and spread out
flat, 64c shows it on an actual Greek bronze
figure. The size of the garment can be judged
by comparing the flat plan with the garment
in wear, as both are to same scale. To adjust
the garment, it should be pleated into folds at
L, M, N, O, along the dotted lines, and then
slung round the figure, passing under left
armpit, the point *E* in front, and the corresponding point *e* at back should be grasped and

Fig. 67a.

Fig. 67c.

drawn up with the ends of the pleats on to the right shoulder and firmly clasped with a brooch; the other small brooches, A, B, C, D, should then be fastened. Last of all, the over-fold above the pleats should be grasped along the line at x, x, x, x, and gently pulled towards G. This should be done both back and front. The Archaic artists represented this as a stiff frill exaggerating the pretty fussy effect of the over-fold (*see* Figs. 64c and 64d) when treated as described. Fig. 67b shows the older method of wear as in Fig. 69a, p. 68, but here with a coquettish touch the garment is thrown backwards again over the right shoulder. This method was imitated again in the late periods. Fig. 67c from a late fifth-century vase-painting, and representing Epimetheus welcoming the returning Pandora, can be compared with Fig. 42 to demonstrate the difference between the short tunic or chiton in the Doric and Ionic styles respectively. The Ionic dress of Fig. 67c is almost identical with that of the youth at Fig. 44a. Fig. 65 is of the early fifth century B.C., and shows the elaborate folding of the top (seen in Fig. 64a) has changed into a simpler style ; it would be fastened on the shoulder with one clasp only (the clasp being towards the back, as it is not shown in the drawing). This example, from a vase-painting in the British Museum, is fastened on the left shoulder, not the right, as is more usual.

Fig. 66, which is of the fifth-century B.C. Fine Period, shows in the arrangement of the himation the elegant and studied simplicity of this particular era. Contemporaneous

with this figure we have others
wearing the himation similarly,
but with the addition of a simple
over-fold like that of the Doric
chiton all along the top edge
and about eighteen inches in
depth. Fig. 68 which is also
of fifth century B.C., shows
the himation lightly adjusted
to the figure without fastenings
over the left shoulder, under
the right armpit and again
over the left forearm. This
fashion persisted and was extraordinarily popular as late as
the sixth century of the Christian
Era. Besides all these methods
of wear which have been
enumerated, the himation was
frequently used to envelop the

Fig. 68.

entire figure, even covering the head ; this is specially
seen in the fourth and third centuries B.C.   No dimensions
are fixed for the garment.   As has been said it was always
rectangular in shape, and its measurements vary in size
and proportions.

GREEK MALE COSTUME

There is great similarity between Greek male and female
dress.   The Doric and Ionic chiton with or without the
covering himation were worn.   Examples of Greek male
costume have been already illustrated at Figs. 42, 44a, 53 and

Fig. 69a.   Fig. 70a.   Fig. 71.

58c, but there are several additional points to be noted.
On elderly men and on ceremonial occasions the tunic
fell to the feet, but for younger men and manual workers
it reached only to mid-thigh, and was often unclasped on
the right shoulder to admit of greater freedom of movement,
as at Fig. 42.   The himation was at times worn without
the chiton under it, and frequently in this case was of great
size so that it covered the figure to the feet.   The simplest
method of arranging the himation or *chlamys* is shown in
wear in Fig. 69a (dating sixth century B.C., and is a representation of the god Hermes in his characteristic traveller's
hat [*petasos*] and boots).   This cloak is simply thrown over
the shoulders and either hangs loose or is held by the hands in
front.   It is here worn over a chiton.   Fig. 69b shows a
fifth-century B.C. representation of the same subject as the

Fig. 70b.   Fig. 69b.

sixth-century 69a. The god Hermes is now represented as
a handsome youth instead of the strong bearded man of the
earlier version. His short cloak (*chlamys*) is fastened on the
right shoulder. His tunic is thin and of that finely pleated
or crinkled material characteristic of later Ionic dress.
Again at Fig. 70b we have the figure of the god Zeus clad
in the himation or large cloak and here it forms his
entire costume and is exceedingly ample. The date of
Fig. 70b is later in the fifth century B.C. than that of Fig. 70a

Fig. 72.

with which it can be compared. It will be seen that these two figures are wearing the himation draped in a not dissimilar mode save that in the one case it is worn over a tunic and in the other it alone forms the entire costume. Fig. 71 (dating fifth century B.C.) shows the travelling costume of a century later ; the hat (*petasos*) has taken a different form, and the cloak, a larger oblong (in proportion practically a double square), is now fastened on the right shoulder by a brooch, and the fantastic boots are replaced by an arrangement of leather thongs following closely the line of foot and limb. This cloak, as shown in Fig. 71, was generally given the name of " chlamys," though there is little difference, except that the chlamys may be smaller, between it and the himation. The Fig. 70a (early fifth century B.C.) shows a dignified draping of the himation for men. One end is laid over the left shoulder and the garment is then drawn round the back, under the right armpit, and then thrown backwards over the left shoulder as shown in the drawing.

Fig. 73.

GREEK ARMOUR

Like the armour of Mediaeval Europe that of the Greeks has a literature devoted to its study. Besides the well-known classical dictionaries there are numerous works of easy access which deal with the subject both from its literary and technical aspects. While this appears to be outside the scope of the present volume—dealing as it does with costumes and that from the technical point of view—it may, nevertheless, not seem inappropriate to give a few examples of armour, looking at them rather from their silhouette and connection with contemporary civilian dress and leaving their technical aspect to be studied elsewhere. Fig. 72 is an example of Archaic Greek armour. This is from a Corinthian

Fig. 74.

vase-painting in the Louvre (Paris) and already exhibits the helmet, corselet or cuirass and greaves which with the somewhat large circular shield forms the typical defensive equipment of the Greek soldier of the later centuries.

A second Archaic example, Fig. 73, is from that well-known relief, " The Stele of Aristion," now in the National Museum, Athens.   Here we have a representation in clear detail of an Athenian " Hoplite " or heavy-armed foot soldier.   He wears a close-fitting Attic helmet without neck-piece, a metal corselet with metal shoulder-pieces, below the waist there is a species of pleated leather kilt to defend the lower part of the body.   Underneath his body-armour he has a linen tunic which appears draping the thighs and upper arm.   He wears the usual greaves and his feet, as was customary with the Greek soldier, are bare.   Fig. 74 is a

Fig. 75.   Fig. 76.   Fig. 77.

Fig. 78.

drawing copied from Hope's *Costume of the Ancients*.
Hope describes it as being taken " from a fictile vase " and
as representing two " Greek Combatants separated by a
Herald." This is interesting as it gives a clear back-view
of one of the figures who is also bearing a very ancient

example of a heraldic device upon his shield. Another point of interest is the costume of the herald. He wears a very early type of the herald's " tabard " with which the mediaeval art of Europe has made us so familiar. This garment is possibly of leather or, alternatively, of padded woven material. Greek armour of the fifth and fourth centuries B.C. is represented with great frequency in the vase-paintings. There are variations (especially in the helmets); Fig. 75 from a vase-painting is an additional example. There is a detailed description of Greek armour in the British Museum guide-book to Greek and Roman life.

The Phrygian dress represented in Fig. 77 suggests, by its tightly fitted silhouette, an origin of leather, knitted or even felted material. This drawing represents a female warrior, one of the so-called Amazons. In the chapter on " Ancient Persian Costume " in Vol. I. we note fitted garments of somewhat similar type, and on p. 15 of this present volume a Cretan costume shows a tight-fitting bodice with a skirt of the undressed skin of some animal pointing to the probable origin of all early *fitted* types of dress in *leather*. The Greek vase-paintings have many examples of male and female figures in these attractive Phrygian costumes similar to that of Fig. 77, and some will also be found in Hope's *Costume of the Ancients*. Fig. 78, which Hope describes as " a Phrygian Lady " (she is in fact Deinomache, and in his illustration she is seen accompanying Hippolyte, Queen of the Amazons, into battle), is a fine example. The celebrated Phrygian cap (the " Cap of Liberty ") and the graceful tight-fitting dress, which may be of very supple leather or possibly soft thick woollen material, are decorated with what is probably embroidery applied with a highly developed sense of proportion and restraint. As a complete contrast take Fig. 79 ; another example of costume which in this case is certainly of leather as opposed to woven draperies. This is from the decoration in relief of an Electrum vase by a Greek artist of the fourth century B.C. It represents a Scythian warrior—a bowman. He wears a cap or hood, tunic and

Fig. 79.

trousers, all of leather as are also his high soft boots. He carries a second bow in the quiver, which is slung on to his body. The original is now in the Historical Museum at Moscow, it was found in a grave in South Russia. The costume may be said to be in partial contrast to Greek draperies. Fig. 76 is that of a Maenad taken from a vase-painting in the British Museum (mid fifth century B.C.). Her elaborately draped Ionic dress is surmounted by the skin of a leopard slung round the waist and over one shoulder and tied at the back. Another mode of wearing the skin was to tie two of the legs round the neck and let the skin hang down the back like a cloak. In Homeric times a lion's or leopard's skin was worn by the warrior. We read of Agamemnon and Menelaus thus clothed.

GREEK ORNAMENT

The details of Greek ornament are familiar to all, as they have been copied first by the Romans, and afterwards

by Renaissance ornamental designers. We can classify the
types which were specially applied to costume into five main
divisions. The types of ornament used on costume were
often decided upon owing to the methods of their application,
which are, broadly speaking, three. A *woven ornament*, which
may be subdivided into (*a*1) *darned or tapestry woven patterns*,
chiefly borders ; (*a*2) *all-over woven patterns*. While the
tapestry woven patterns were often geometric, we also find
human figures and animals. The all-over woven patterns
(*a*2) were usually geometric.

The second method of application (*b*) was that of *dye-
painting*, and as this admitted of great freedom of execution
the patterns were applied more lavishly and with a certain
breadth of style. We find borders, such as the " wave
pattern " and the " egg and tongue " (both common in
architecture and in vase-painting), executed on textiles,

Fig. 80.   Fig. 81.

and these borders may edge figure-subjects, animals and foliage. The third method (*c*) of application was that of *embroidery*. The well-known " palmette " pattern was a favourite motif for this, the delicate stems and spirals lending themselves well to needlework. Some fragments of Greek materials were found on the site of an ancient Greek colony at Kertch in the Crimea, and these have been assigned to the fifth or fourth century B.C. One is of violet woollen cloth

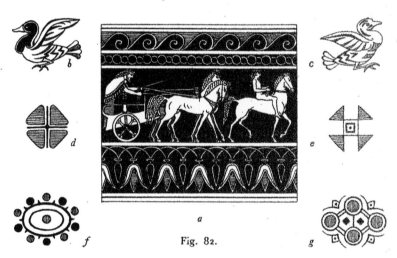

Fig. 82.

embroidered with a " palmette " pattern in gold and green of similar type to Fig. *g* in Plate III. A painted cloth from the same site has patterns similar to Figs. *c* and *d*.

The five types of Greek ornament on Plate III. may be classified as follows :

1. Frets and other patterns based on them, examples *a* and *b*.
2. The " wave " or " spiral " pattern, the " egg and tongue " pattern, examples *c* and *d* (with these may be mentioned the " bead and reel " pattern and the " waterleaf ").
3. Leaf and flower and berry borders (as in *e*, *f* and *j*), bay and ivy (the favourites).

4. The " palmette " patterns. These are, perhaps, the most widely
used after the Archaic period. Fig. *g* is an example.

5. Bands of animals or human figures sometimes divided by blocks
of the fret patterns; *h* and *i* are examples of this type. Other examples
have the figures in continuous bands, at times representing scenes of war
or festive processions. The patterns on the vase-paintings of the sixth
century B.C. show figures wearing these elaborately patterned garments,
but in the fifth and fourth centuries B.C. we find the lighter floral patterns
and the decoration (with the exception of a small geometric all-over
pattern) confined to the border of the garment only. On p. 76 are shown
Figs. 80 and 81, two decorated dresses of the fourth century B.C., and on
page 77, Fig. 82*a*, the over-fold of a dress of the richly decorated Archaic
style.

Fig. 82*a*, the over-fold of a sixth-century B.C. woman's
dress, cut as that shown on Fig. 36*a*, p. 43. The entire dress
is covered with similar bands, the ornamental bands alter-
nating with those of figures and animals. Some examples
of this type show bands of figures and animals only.

Figs. 82*b* and *c* are from one of the fifth-century B.C.
fragments of textiles found at Kertch, a Greek colony in
South Russia. The birds are disposed in alternate bands
over the fabric.

Figs. 82*d* to *g* are examples of Greek ornament of sixth
century B.C., and are taken from vase-paintings.

Figs. 83*a*, *b*, *c* and *g* show four types of hairdressing in
addition to those seen on the costumes already illustrated.
Figs. 83*a* and *c* are both from the heads of mourners and both
taken from Hope's *Costume of the Ancients*, which describes
83*a* as the head of Electra with her hair shorn in token of
her grief. While at Fig. 83*c* the mourner expresses her
sorrow by veiling her head with a fold of her himation.
Fig. 83*b* is from the sculptured head of a youth dating *c*.
480 B.C. and now in the Museum of the Acropolis at Athens.
Here we see the typical mode of hairdressing of the young
athlete of the early fifth century. In a later age, after 480

PLATE III.—GREEK ORNAMENT.

Fig. 83.

B.C., the Greek youth wore his hair short. Fig. 83*g*, from a bronze head of Zeus found at Olympia and dating sixth century B.C., shows clearly the more elaborate style of hair-dressing of this age ; the curled fringe on the forehead is not unlike that of an Assyrian king of the same period, and the method· of looping and binding the hair behind the head goes back to a far earlier era. There is a suggestion of this method of binding on the hair of Fig. 32 (seventh century B.C.) and also with that on the seal-impression from Ur in Mesopotamia *c.* 2000 B.C. (*see* Fig. 31*e*). In the original bronze head of Fig. 83*g* the lower parts of neck and shoulders are missing ; they have been supplied here from an early vase-painting.

A point to be noted with regard to male hairdressing,

in the later periods is, that while young boys in Sparta wore their hair short and grew it on reaching manhood, the custom at Athens was the reverse, boys wore long hair while young and on reaching manhood it was cut off and dedicated in a temple.   The hairdressing of the Greek women before the fifth century B.C. was comparatively simple.   It varied from the free-flowing locks, similar to those seen in the Aegean styles to the looped and bound-up hair already

Fig. 84.   Fig. 86.   Fig. 85.

described as having its origin in Mesopotamian examples as early as 2000 B.C.   During the latter part of the fifth century the women drew back their waved hair and dressed it in a simple knot behind the head, sometimes confining it with net or band, but in later ages, as in the fourth century B.C., the styles became immensely varied as can be seen from a study of the vase-paintings of the period.   The various dictionaries of Classical Antiquities show many examples of these late styles in hairdressing, and there are numerous illustrations in Hope's *Costume of the Ancients.*

Figs. 83*d* and *e* show portions of two gold necklaces which are typically Greek in design and characteristic especially of the fifth century B.C. These designs, however, are by no means original, the elements—rosette, lotus flower and bud etc., are clearly borrowed from Egyptian sources.

Fig. 87.

Figs. 83*f* and *h*, drawings of the Attic and Corinthian helmets from Hope's *Costume of the Ancients*, are here given so that the two can be easily compared. The Attic helmet with its hinged cheek-pieces is a much more practical head-piece than the Corinthian which, when pulled down over the face, allows of a very limited field of vision through its eye-holes. Compare Figs. 74 and 40*b* with Figs. 83*f* and *h* when the helmets can be seen in wear and off the head respectively.

CHILDREN'S DRESS

While it can hardly be said that there was any distinctive dress for children among the Greeks, Figs. 84 to 87 show a few typical examples. Fig. 84 from a memorial relief (Stele) of a young girl shows a costume which might equally well have been worn by a grown woman and the same may be said of the hairdressing. The costume is of a fifth-century B.C. Doric type ; compare with Fig. 35.

Fig. 85 from a vase *c.* 480 B.C. (now in Berlin Museum) shows a schoolboy wrapped in an ample himation, which is draped to cover the figure entirely. This was the correct wear for a boy receiving a lesson from his teacher. When, however, the subject was that of instruction in music the pupil allowed his himation to fall to the waist while he sat in front of his master who was in similar garb, each of them with a lyre on his knee.

Figs. 86 and 87 may perhaps be called genuine children's frocks ; they are from vases of the fourth century B.C. now in the British Museum. At Fig. 86 we see a girl of about eight years old receiving instruction in dancing.

At Fig. 87 a small boy of perhaps four or five years of age is at play. Round his neck is slung a species of hoop to which are attached various tops, chiefly rattles (*crepundia*). The little tunic is cut on the usual T-shaped plan of all sleeved costumes of this period in the civilized world except when the material was leather. Here the somewhat conventional drawing suggests the appearance of fitting or shaping ; this is probably not the case, but the sleeves certainly seem to be of thinner stuff than the body-part. One feels that these two little embroidered tunics may have come from abroad, perhaps from Phrygia, a country famed for its embroidery in fine wools, the name " opus Phrygianus " being a synonym for embroidery in ancient times.

With the technical aspect of the shaping of Greek dress, as explained in this chapter, thoroughly understood the student can gain a wider knowledge of the beauty and variety seen in Greek costume-designing by consulting the numerous books on Greek art which can be found in most public libraries. There, upon the two simple themes of the Doric and Ionic, an infinite number of changes are worked out, and can be recognized on the noble sculptures of the fifth century B.C. as well as on the simplest Archaic vase-painting.

ANCIENT ROMAN COSTUME

BEFORE describing the dress of Republican and Imperial
Rome it will be of interest to examine a few types of dress
as worn by the peoples inhabiting the Italian peninsula
previous to this great era. The names of the Latins, Volscians,
Samnites and, above all, the Etruscans are familiar in this
connection, but it is chiefly to the numerous remains of the
art of the Etruscans that we are indebted for our knowledge
of what may be called pre-Roman Costume. The influence
of Greek civilization upon the art of the Etruscans and
indeed of that of the Samnites is strongly in evidence but
in the representations of costume certain details appear
which are clearly non-Greek. The Etruscans, we are told,
were probably emigrants from Asia Minor, and their high
boots, often with turned-up toes, are seen in almost identical
form in the ancient Hittite sculptures. A glance at Fig. 88,
which is from an ancient Assyrian bas-relief now in the
British Museum and dating 880 B.C., will show again that
this Asiatic costume has points of resemblance to Figs. 89
and 90. Fig. 89 is taken from an Etruscan tomb-painting
(Tomba dell'Orco fourth century B.C.). Figs. 90 and 91
are from an Etruscan wall-painting now in the British
Museum, the date is 600 B.C. The high boots worn by
Fig. 91 have their counterpart in those worn by the woman

Fig. 88.   Fig. 89.   Fig. 90.

at Fig. 90, as another female figure in the same fresco
with skirt held up most clearly shows. Our knowledge of
Etruscan costume is chiefly derived from the numerous
tomb-paintings which have been unearthed and carefully
described, and also from statuettes in bronze and terra-cotta
effigies.

Figs. 92, 93 and 94 are from Etruscan tomb-paintings
of early fifth century B.C. The women's dresses appear to
be cut on similar lines to those of ancient Greece, but some
authorities consider that triangular gores may have been
introduced into the lower portion of the tunics to give the
wide-skirted effect. The unusual decoration of wreaths of
flowers round the arms, at the shoulder of Fig. 92, are remarkable. Fig. 93 wears a miniature toga of semi-circular
or segmental shape ; one extremity hangs outwards over the
right arm, the deepest part of the curve covers the front of

Fig. 91.   Fig. 92.   Fig. 93.

the body, the remainder of the drapery is thrown over the left elbow, drawn across the back and thrown forwards over the right shoulder; this last throw is not seen in the drawing. Fig. 94 wears the high Etruscan cap (*tutulus*) which is said to have originally come from the east by way of Cyprus. The ornament at Fig. 95 is taken from a tomb wall-painting, and illustrates the influence of Greek art upon Etruscan, showing, as it does, the well-known Greek motif of dolphins over the waves in the form of a border pattern. Fig. 96 is taken from a bronze statuette of the close of the sixth century B.C. The Greek and Asiatic influences are clearly to be seen in this costume. If the tunic and small shoulder-wrap be compared with those of the Archaic Greek goddess from Attica at Fig. 67a, Chapter II., the similarity is evident; on the other hand the high cap and the boots resemble those

Fig. 94.

seen on the costumes of the figures in Hittite sculptured reliefs. We have many examples of Etruscan armour depicted in the tomb-paintings and also in sculpture. There the similarity with Greek armour is striking, helmet, cuirass and greaves often almost identical in the two styles. Fig. 97, however—a Samnite warrior, from a fifth-century B.C. bronze statue, now in the Louvre, Paris—shows a short tight tunic (which may be of leather) and a metal breast-plate with bosses differing from the Greek warriors' equipment, while his greaves and helmet, on the other hand, do resemble those of Ancient Greece.

ROMAN COSTUME

For convenience the traditional date of the foundation of Rome (753 B.C.) may be taken as a beginning, and the style may be said to have merged gradually into " Byzantine " about the fifth century A.D.

Fig. 95.

The Etruscan costumes illustrated at Figs. 89–97 may be taken as illustrative of an early period of the dress of Southern and Central Italy, but the chief and most distinctive feature of Roman costume in Republican and Imperial times—the toga —had a very early origin. At first the toga was a semi-circular garment of moderate size, and was the characteristic dress of both men and women in the seventh and sixth centuries B.C. After this period the influence of Greece upon Italian costume became so strong that Roman costumes, in the case of women, grew to be almost identical with Greek, and in the case of men, always excepting the toga, the similarity was marked.

Fig. 96.

Fig. 97.

Before describing Roman costume generally it will therefore seem most desirable that the toga should be fully explained. While its mode of wear in the early centuries was simple and easily understood, the highly elaborate methods of draping which were practised from the first century B.C. until the fifth century A.D. require a most careful attention if they are to be apprehended. A glance at the three figures 98, 99 and 100 will show the three characteristic toga styles—

Fig. 98.   Fig. 99.   Fig. 100.

early, middle and late—the draping of which is described herewith. Fig. 98, Roman or Etruscan example dating 200 B.C., is a statue generally called " The Orator," and is now in the museum at Florence. Fig. 99 is a portrait statue of the Emperor Titus, A.D. 79–81, while Fig. 100 is from a statue of a Roman magistrate of the fourth century A.D. By far the best method of study is to cut out the garment and drape it according to the written description and explanatory diagrams, such as are given in this volume. The illustrations on the next page, Figs. 101a to 101f, are taken from an Etruscan bronze statuette of early fifth century B.C. in the British Museum. The plan of the garment, i.e. the segment of a circle, is shown to a small scale at 101c, and it is decorated with a pattern, 101d, *around the curved edge,* whereas in later times the straight edge was the decorated

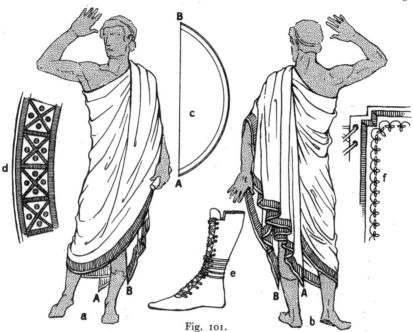

Fig. 101.

one. The method of adjusting is to allow the end *B* to hang
down in front over the left shoulder, keeping the straight
edge nearest the neck, then pass the garment round back
of shoulders, under right armpit, across chest and throw
the end *A* backwards over the left shoulder. *A* hangs
down the back as illustrated. This toga would measure
about sixteen feet along the straight edge and about six feet
deep in centre. The figure wears a pair of high laced
boots, Fig. 101*e*, which are decorated with a border,
diagram 101*f*. A loin-cloth was usually worn underneath
before the tunic came into vogue as an undergarment for
the toga.

The fully developed toga of Republican and Imperial
Rome was in shape the segment of a circle and about eighteen

and a half feet long by seven feet deep at its centre. It was decorated at times by a stripe along its straight edge. This type
is seen in wear on the Emperor Titus at Fig. 99, where the
head is uncovered; and again in wear with the head covered
(as in the diagram Fig. 102,) at Fig. 120 from the Ara Pacis,
while the baby boy, Fig. 124, in this latter illustration, wears
his toga after the manner of the Emperor Titus. In the illustrations 102a and 102b, the method of draping is as follows
(Diagram 102c). Take a point on the straight edge A B about
one-third of its length from A. Place this point on the left
shoulder. Allow point A to fall to the ground in front, then
carry the remainder of the straight edge round the back of
shoulders and underneath the right arm. Now grasp the garment at a point (x) about one-third or more of its depth from
the straight edge and allow a flap or over-fold to hang down.
Gather and twist some folds at the right side of waist-line
to form a belt (baltaeus) and tuck the point x well into the
girdle of the tunic underneath ; this keeps it in place. Now
let the over-fold already formed droop towards the knee in a
curve and throw the remainder of the garment backwards
over the left shoulder, letting the end B hang down towards
the feet. The semi-circular over-fold now seen was called
the sinus. The last stage of draping is that of forming the
boss, or umbo. This is done by pulling up a portion of that
part of the toga which was first allowed to fall to the ground
in front. The result is to lift the end A off the ground a few
inches and to give the characteristic small drapery hanging
out over the left side of waist-line and ascending to the left
shoulder. The model at Fig. 102 has lifted up the sinus or
over-fold to form a head-covering, as was done for certain
religious ceremonies, but for general use the over-fold hung
down from the shoulders at the back. This model is wearing

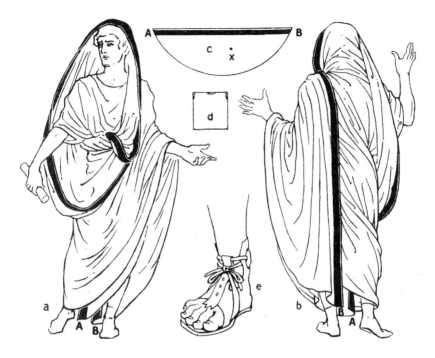

Fig. 102.

a sleeveless tunic (*tunica*) reaching to the elbows and to the knees. The tunic is shown to a small scale and in correct proportion to the toga at 102*d*. He also wears a pair of low half-boots (*crepida*) which leave the toes uncovered, Fig. 102*e*. The material of the toga was almost invariably wool of the natural colour and was not decorated ; this was the proper dress of the Roman citizen and denoted his status. The statue of the Emperor Marcus Aurelius (A.D. 161-180), in the British Museum, wears a similar draping except that the sinus fold is not lifted to cover the head.

This method of draping the toga was in vogue from about the second century B.C. till the second century A.D.

Among the many styles of toga, the following may be noted :

1. Toga *pura* or *virilis*, ordinary dress of Roman citizen, undecorated, natural colour wool.

2. Toga *praetexta*, worn by youths under sixteen years of age, and also by magistrates ; white, with a band of purple or scarlet along the straight edge.

3. Toga *pulla*, black or dark coloured, for mourning.

4. Toga *candida*, white and plain, worn by candidates for public office.

5. Toga *picta*, worn by victorious generals, and later by emperors and consuls ; purple, gold embroidered.

6. Toga *trabea*, bright scarlet stripes and a purple hem, worn by augurs.

7. Toga *cinctus Gabinus*, the baltaeus passed twice round waist instead of over left shoulder and so leaving left arm free.

8. Toga *contabulatum*, worn folded along the straight edge as illustrated on Figs. 100, 103a and b, 104a and b, and Figs. 138a, b and c.

Fig. 100 shows a " toga contabulatum " in wear. Here the garment seems to be of segmental shape but small in size and the draping as follows : With straight edge uppermost, place centre of toga in right armpit, draw over chest and back to left and secure in place with a band or girdle arranging a number of pleats at left armpit. Let the front point of toga hang down outwards over left forearm and draw up the back point forwards over the left shoulder, tucking it into the girdle under the right armpit and at the same time arranging this end in a wide band or set of folds. These folded drapings are seen in great variety, a few of them are described herewith.

At the commencement of the second century A.D. the toga was going out of fashion as the ordinary dress of a Roman citizen, but as a ceremonial costume it was retained, and as late as the fifth century A.D. we find it worn by Roman consuls and highly ornamented (*toga picta*). Figs. 103a and 103b show the garment as worn by the Consul Flavius Felix, A.D. 428. The dimensions of this toga are

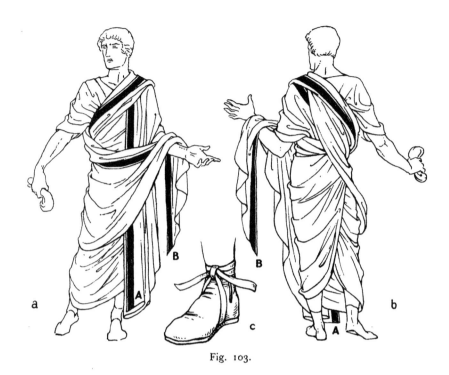

Fig. 103.

longer and narrower than that of the Republican Era, though the shape is similar except that an eight-inch ornamental band was probably sewn to the straight edge. The straight edge of this example is about twenty-one feet and the depth at centre of segment about six feet. The method of draping is as follows : Begin by making toga into folds of about eight inches wide and arrange them so that the stripe will show. Wind one end (*A*) backwards from the wrist to shoulder of left arm so that the arm is entirely covered. This forms a shield or protection to the arm, and the toga, if worn while fighting, was thus draped ; it also serves to hold this first portion of the toga out of the way until the complete draping is made. Now

pass over the left shoulder and draw it downwards across
the back until it rests at right side of waist, and, having
sufficiently loosened the folds to allow the curved edge to
reach the ankles, draw the straight edge onwards across the
front of waist, still keeping it in folds to prevent trailing.
Continue round the back of waist until the right side is
reached again.   Now take the whole garment and throw
upwards across the chest and over the left shoulder, taking
care to display the band.   Draw downwards across the back
to the right side again.   Now unwind the portion of toga
from the left arm and allow it to hang down to the feet from
the left shoulder.   Last of all, take the still undraped portion
of the toga and throw it across the front of the body and
across the crook of the left elbow, the left arm being bent
at a right angle to thus receive it.   The end B hangs down
on the outer side of the left elbow as shown in diagram.
This form of draping gives an opening at the back of the
legs and admits of movement, such as would be required
when mounting a horse and riding.   To ensure further
convenience, the two ends A and B can be wound round
the waist and tucked in.*   The great thickness of this draping
over the chest, waist and loins made the toga into a species
of defensive cuirass, and the phrase " armed with the toga "
has been used to describe it.   Diagram 103c is an illustration of
the Roman boot, or calceus.   It had a slit at each side of the ankle
to allow the foot to enter, and was kept in place by thongs
of leather, as shown in the drawing.   It was of untanned
leather with black thongs, but patricians wore red boots.

One of the latest and most elaborate methods of draping
the toga is shown on the figure of the Consul Manlius
Boethius, A.D. 487 (Fig. 104).   It forms a complete covering

* Thus tucked in, this would be an example of No. 7, " Cinctus Gabinus."

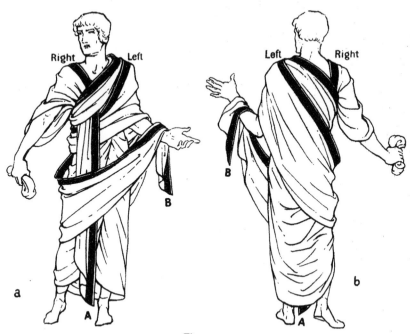

Fig. 104.

for the figure, though, in the case of this consul, a long-sleeved full-length tunic is worn underneath, as is seen in wear at Fig. 100. Heuzey suggests that this elaborate draping and the one described at Fig. 104 may really be survivals of some archaic method of wearing the toga. The garment as worn by Manlius Boethius is still longer and narrower than the last example, and would be about twenty-four feet long by four and a half feet deep in the centre; it would have the same segmental shape as the ordinary toga, but the curve, of course, very much flatter, and, like the last example, a wide ornamental band sewn along the straight edge. To drape this example as shown, Figs. 104a and 104b, begin by winding backwards one end of the toga, A, round the right arm to keep it out of the way, then starting from under the right armpit draw the drapery down to centre of waist in front, give the whole garment a double twist, and then let the straight edge lie along the waist and the curved hang down till it touches the left ankle. Draw the garment, still in the same position, round the back of waist to the centre front again and give it another double twist. The legs are now clothed with a drapery which should slightly overlap in front and drape the limbs fully at back. It should be sufficiently loose to admit of walking freely. After the last twist, keep the garment folded into about eight inches wide with the ornamental band showing, and draw round the waist towards the left across the back of waist and under the right armpit, then still in band-form over the left shoulder. Now let the folds hang somewhat looser and repeat this last draping again, so that there are two diagonal drapings running from right side of waist, across chest and over left shoulder. Still continue winding the toga round the figure in the same direction, but let it fall to the right hip or lower and throw the end B loosely across the front of figure and over the left elbow, held bent to receive it, as in the case of the example at Fig. 103. Last of all, unwind the end A from the right arm and interlace it under the top fold over the second and under the last, as shown in the diagram. The end A falls over the front opening of the drapery. Care should be taken that the band decorating the straight edge is always fully displayed.

SUMMARY OF GARMENTS OTHER THAN THE TOGA WORN BY ROMAN MEN

1. The *tunica*, with or without sleeves. *With* sleeves, a T-shape ; *without* them a simple rectangle. When sleeveless it differed from the Greek tunic, inasmuch as the armholes were at the sides, not at the top. It varied in length and in width, just as did the Greek, and the sleeves

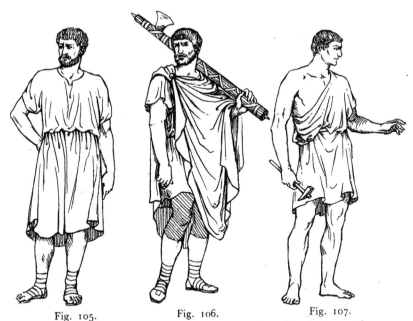

Fig. 105.   Fig. 106.   Fig. 107.

when worn varied from a few inches to wrist length. If more than one
tunica was worn, that underneath was called the *tunica interior*. The
garment was usually plain wool or linen and in some cases decorated
by one stripe (*clavus*) down centre front and back, or two (*clavi*), down
each side of front and back, as seen on the Etruscan man's figure at Fig.
89. These two stripes became the distinguishing badge of knights or
cavalrymen during the centuries preceding the Christian Era, but later
they again lost their significance and became purely decorative. They
were tapestry darned into the material in wools of a purple, indigo or
deep wine colour. The *tunica palmata* was richly embroidered all over
in gold on a purple silk ground ; it was worn thus by Roman Emperors
and later by consuls. The *tunica talaris* reached to the ankles. The
working-classes wore the tunic short, a few inches above the knee, or
knee length, also sleeveless and girded at the waist. Fig. 105 illustrates
the typical dress of a Roman " plebian " or man of the common people,
his *tunica* appears to have short sleeves. For all strenuous work the right
arm was withdrawn from the garment, leaving the shoulder bare and
arm free. *See* Fig. 107. This example (Fig. 107) is taken from the figure
in a Roman relief representing a working cutler with his hammer at
a forge (British Museum).

2. The *colobium* (from the Greek *kolobos*, docked or curtailed) was
a variety of the *tunica* with short or curtailed sleeves. It was worn by

Roman men of free birth and was the first dress adopted by Christian deacons who later wore the *dalmatic*. The dates of the *tunica* and *colobium* extend from the commencement of the Roman Era until the third century A.D. or later. It will be gathered from this description that there is practically no distinction in shape between the *tunica* and *colobium*, Fig. 105 will illustrate either garment in wear. At the same time the *colobium* of the later centuries was certainly a much wider and more voluminous garment than the *tunica*, see Fig. 139.

3. The *abolla*, a rectangular woollen cloak of about four feet by eight feet, worn folded double and fastened with a brooch on the right shoulder. It was worn by officers in the army and generally red in colour. In the illustration Fig. 106, it is shown as worn by a Roman " lictor " carrying the " fasces " over his shoulder. It will be noticed that Fig. 106 is wearing short trousers or breeches under his tunic. This was really a fashion borrowed from the men of Gaul and adopted by legionary soldiers and others occasionally for wear in cold climates. The Romans named these garments *braccae*. In this example also the *abolla* is not doubled, but worn in single folds.

4. The *birrus* or *burrus*, a rectangular cloak or cape with a hood (*cucullus*) attached. It was made of thick coarse wool, and worn in bad weather.

5. The *lacerna*, a rectangular cloak, with rounded corners, worn over the toga as an extra wrap, and fastened to the shoulder by a brooch (*fibula*) ; it had a hood and was an expensive garment of thin fine wool, and often brightly coloured.

6. The *laena*, a very thick, rectangular, woollen cloak with a shaggy nap on both sides, used for very cold weather, sometimes red in colour. Fig. 108 is that of a shepherd from a relief now in the Mus. delle Terme and dating A.D. 124. Here we have the tunic as in Fig. 105 but considerably shorter and wider, also a cloak which may possibly be the *laena* worn along with the characteristic hat (the Greek *petasos*) and high boots. The similarity in dress here with that of the Greek shepherd of previous centuries and with that of his mediaeval counterpart again, centuries later, is remarkable.

7. The *paenula*, a semi-circular cloak fastened up the front and often with a hood attached, worn by men and women for travel, also by countryfolk in place of the toga ; also worn by slaves. It was dark in colour and usually wool, though occasionally of fur. It varies slightly in shape, being sometimes almost circular, and comparable to the South American " poncho," the Moorish " burnous " (Fig. 109), and the Cossack " burka."

8. The *paludamentum*. The military cloak worn by officers, as distinguished from the *sagum* worn by the rank and file of the army. Properly it is the cloak which was put on by a Roman general when leaving the city for a campaign, and was doffed when he re-entered. It was rectangular, and larger and thicker than the *sagum* ; it was worn with a clasp on the right shoulder like the *abolla*. In colour it was usually purple.

9. The *pallium*, a rectangular mantle or shawl identical with the Greek himation. The Romans were familiar with it, but seldom wore it, regarding it as distinctively Greek, and therefore not patriotic for their own wear.

10. The *sagum*, a thick woollen cloak similar to the *abolla* and fastened round the neck with a brooch, generally red ; it was the distinctive badge not only of the soldier, but of the Roman citizen in time of war (*see* Fig. 117). Here the garment is wound round the left arm in similar fashion to the more voluminous *paludamentum* worn by the Emperor Hadrian, Fig. 111a.

Fig. 108.

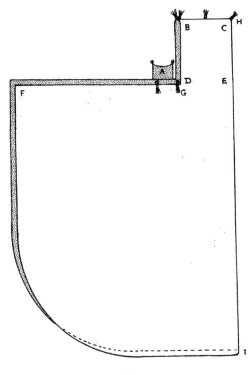

Fig. 109.

Besides the *cucullus*, or hood, the Roman men had a felt conical cap called the *pilleus*, and the Greek *petasos* (*see* Fig. 108) was occasionally worn. In the main they went bareheaded. Up till about 300 B.C. beards and long hair were worn ; afterwards, till the time of Hadrian, who reintroduced the beard, a clean-shaven face and short hair was the rule, and the

Fig. 110.

hair was generally combed down all round from the crown of the head and worn in a short fringe across the forehead.

Besides the three examples of men's footgear already given, there was a low boot similar to the *calceus*, but without the thongs, fastened only with a short lace and slit down the front instead of at the sides ; this was called the *pero* and worn by peasants. The thongs of the *calceus* were sometimes long enough to wind round the leg as far as the centre of the calf. Sandals similar to the Greek were used for indoor wear.

In Fig. 109 *A* is for fastening at neck in front. *B, C, D, E* is the hood in side view, *H-I* the centre line of back of garment and *F-G* the centre front. This plan is taken from a Moorish burnous.

Roman Armour and Military Costume

The subject of Roman military costume and armour being of great magnitude and complexity is, of necessity, one which cannot be adequately treated in the present volume, but information is fortunately easily accessible ; *see* bibliography at the end of this volume for work on the subject, also consult the various dictionaries of Classical Antiquities. Only a few typical examples are here given, but these are of a representative character. Fig. 110 is from Trajan's Column, and depicts a Roman legionary soldier ; his helmet has hinged cheek-pieces which can be fastened

under the chin with a thong of
leather. Over his tunic he wears
a short leather jacket strengthened
with metal bands, as shown in
illustration. His shield has the
device of a thunderbolt painted
upon it. Fig. 111*a* is from a
statue of the Emperor Hadrian
(in the British Museum). His
helmet would be of similar shape
to that of the legionary, but
more delicately formed, probably
richly decorated in similar
fashion to his body armour,
and with an upstanding horse-
hair crest. Over his tunic
he wears a metal cuirass,

Fig. 111*a*.

moulded
accurately to the figure. It is
in two pieces, and the back is
hinged to the front under the
right arm, and fastened with
clasps under the left. The
shoulders are joined with metal
hasps hinged to the back piece
and tied down with leather
thongs through holes in the
front piece. The decoration of
the front is a figure-subject in
high relief with the Medusa's head
in addition, as shown in drawing.
Fringed leather straps attached

Fig. 111*b* and *c*.

to the metal protect the shoulders and the thighs, and the high boots are shown in detail, Figs. 111*b* and *c*. The *paludamentum* is twisted out of the way over left shoulder and arm. Armour of similar type but less ornate would be worn by a Roman military commander. The cuirass frequently had a waist-belt or sash to keep back and front more firmly together, and sometimes, instead of the solid metal back and front piece, the whole garment was made of leather with overlapping metal scales (*squamata*) taking the place of breast and back plates. For cuirass or *lorica* see notes in Smith's *Dictionary of Greek and Roman Antiquities*, and for an example of the armour with metal scales see Fig. 117. Figs. 112, 113 and 114 are from Hope's *Costume of the Ancients*; Figs. 112 and 114 show two soldiers armed in similar fashion to Fig. 110. Each of these men is wearing the trousers (*braccae*) which are also seen at Fig. 106. The armour of Fig. 113 resembles that worn by the Emperor Hadrian (Fig. 111*a*). The Gladiators, introduced in the third century B.C. and increased in the second century B.C., though not soldiers, cannot be omitted when describing the armour of the Romans. A victorious gladiator of that special grade or class known as the " Samnites " is shown at Fig. 115. (The origin of the name is due to the fact that the ancient Samnite warriors (*see* Fig. 97) were renowned for their bravery). The " Samnite " Gladiators are described as wearing a high crested helmet, with visor and cheek-pieces. The right arm and left thigh are protected with a strapping of leather. In the illustration Fig. 115 two greaves are shown, but as a rule the Samnite Gladiator had a greave on the left leg only. The oblong shield and short sword are the characteristic Samnite weapons of defence and offence, while the only clothing consists of a lion-cloth

Fig. 112.   Fig. 113.   Fig. 114.

(*subligaculum*) which at times took the form of short drawers, but at Fig. 115 appears to consist of an oblong piece of

stuff with the addition of a triangular apron attached to one end. The rectangular end would be gathered under the belt at the back of the waist, then the remainder would be passed between the legs and drawn up under the belt in front, while the triangular apron at the same time would be kept folded down as shown in illustration, giving the loin-cloth a double thickness in front. In the illustration also

Fig. 115.

Fig. 116.   Fig. 117

Fig. 118.

there is visible a small shoulder-guard (*galerus*) which rises above the leather strapping on the right arm. All the different classes and grades of gladiator—such as the " Retiarii " who fought armed with nets—are well described with good illustrations in Smith's *Dictionary of Greek and Roman Antiquities*. A well-known figure in Roman military life was the Standard-bearer (*Signifer*). An example is shown at Fig. 116 which dates second century A.D. The head of the standard-bearer, as will be seen, is covered by the skin of an animal. The name Centurion also rises inevitably to mind in connection with the Roman armies. Fig. 117, dating like Fig. 116 second century A.D., is an example. The Centurion here shown is in parade uniform. He is without his helmet as he is wearing the " Corona Civitas " or wreath of oak leaves, bestowed for bravery in saving the life of a fellow citizen in war. His cuirass is of the scaled type (*squamata*) to which reference has already been made on p. 102 ; the pendant strips of leather seen in Figs. 111a and 113 are also present here. The cloak is probably the " Sagum " (*see* p. 99) wound round the left arm to keep it out of the way. Over the cuirass is worn a decorative arrangement of medallions (*phalerae*), those on the right and left of each of the three rows being designed in pairs. Slung round his neck over the medallions appear two " torques " of Celtic design. In his right hand the Centurion holds his characteristic staff of vine-wood (*vitis*). The greaves are elaborately decorated. A soldier of the celebrated " Praetorian Guard " cannot be omitted from this short description of Roman military costume. Fig. 118 is an example of one of these guards in parade uniform ; it dates first century B.C. and is from a sculpture in high relief now in the Louvre, Paris. In the group of Praetorian Guards from which this figure is taken the costume of the men is by no means identical. The helmets, for example, are similar but the crests

Fig. 119.

or plumes vary from those with six feathers in a row to those seemingly of horse hair, extending right down to the base of the helmet and tapering. It will be seen that the cuirass of Fig. 118 is covered by a tunic. In the Louvre relief the figure next to him has an uncovered cuirass reaching to the waist and continued with a double tier of leather pendants. The next man has a cuirass reaching to the hips and mitred at the bottom like that of the Centurion's (Fig. 117). In minor details again there is still dissimilarity but the general effect is that of a uniform varied only by small differences.

To close this description of the Civil and Military dress

Fig. 120.   Fig. 121.   Fig. 122.   Fig. 123. · Fig. 124. Fig. 125.

of Roman men Fig. 119 gives the characteristic costume of
a victorious Charioteer (*Auriga*). Besides the wreath and
palm branch of the victor we notice over his tunic and round
his thighs the characteristic binding of leather thongs, to
guard from injury in the highly dangerous form of chariot
racing practised by the Romans. A special point to notice
is the curved knife thrust among the leather thongs so that
the reins, worn knotted round the waist, could be cut in an
emergency. The original of the Victorious Charioteer is in
the Vatican Museum.

Dress of Roman Women before the
Third Century a.d.

Before describing the dress of Roman women it will be
of interest to view the costume of men, women and children
as a whole during the Augustan Age, that " golden prime "
in Roman history. The so-called Altar of Peace (*Ara Pacis*),
dedicated in 9 b.c. and now in the Museo delle Terme, Rome,
is adorned with a procession of stately figures of which those
shown at Figs. 120 to 125 have been selected as examples.
These have been identified as members of the family of the
Emperor Augustus, while scholars are by no means unani-
mous regarding the identity of all of these figures. Fig. 120
is probably Agrippa (son-in-law of Augustus); he is wearing
the toga after the manner shown at diagram Fig. 102. To
his drapery clings a small boy, Fig. 121, clad in a tunic (*tunica*)
and wearing round his neck a Celtic necklet or torque. Fig.
122 next to the boy is said to be the Empress herself. She
wears the cloak (*palla*) draped over her head. It can be
seen that her wavy hair is dressed in a simple manner and
that except for the long sleeves of her tunic (*stola*) and her
feet shod in boots the costume might be that of a Greek
woman of the fifth century b.c. Fig. 123 is dressed in a
precisely similar fashion, save that her uncovered head
shows the simple method of hairdressing more clearly and
that she wears a wreath. This lady is said to be the beautiful
Antonia, the baby boy (Fig. 124) who clings to her hand is
her son Germanicus, and her husband, the elder Drusus,
is seen at Fig. 125. Round the neck of the toga-clad baby
boy there hangs, suspended by a ribbon, the " Bulla "
(literally, bubble) a spherical locket which held a luck-
bringing amulet. Its use was originally derived from the

Fig. 126.

Etruscans. It was worn by a free-born Roman boy children from the ninth day after birth until the *toga praetexta* was laid aside at the age of sixteen years (*see* p. 92). The bulla was then consecrated to the Household Gods ("Lares" *see* Fig. 135). Among the poorer classes the bulla was of leather or base metal but among the rich it was of gold; the loop or clasp of a bulla beautifully wrought in gold is shown at Fig. 128*d*. The last costume of this Ara Pacis group—that already described as being of Drusus the elder, father of Germanicus—is seen at Fig. 125. He is wearing the short tunic over an inner one (*tunica interior*). His rather voluminous cloak is probably the *paludamentum* and his head, like that of his wife, is adorned with a wreath in honour of the festival. He wears a pair of sandals of elegant design in place of the more usual boots. Among the many figures seen in this great procession of the Ara Pacis there is one quite near to Drusus of a young girl child of about eight or nine years of age draped in the toga in exactly similar fashion to that shown on the baby boy at Fig. 124, the only indication of girlhood being that the hair, in this case, is done up in a knot at the back of the head. The toga, as has been said (p. 87), was worn by the Etruscans in very early times by both sexes, but in the Roman Era it was not worn by girls or women of good character after childhood; the wearing of the toga by women was a mark of disgrace.

It has been already remarked that the costume of Roman

women was almost identical with
the Greek. The Ionic chiton
and himation were worn, with
slight alterations, and named by
the Romans the *stola* and the
palla respectively.   Underneath
the *stola* was worn the *tunica
interior*. Fig. 126 is that of a
girl of eleven or twelve years of
age from a group of statuary
now at Chatsworth and dating
fifth century A.D.   It well
illustrates the indoor dress of
Roman girls and women and
shows the *stola* and *tunica interior* in
wear.   In the original groups Fig.
126 is standing beside the chair of

Fig. 127.

her mother whose dress is the same with the addition of a
palla, and also we see on the mother the same elaborately
dressed hair shown at Figs. 128*a* and *c* but evidently not
considered a suitable mode for the young girl.   The *stola*
was cut either with or without sleeves ; when with sleeves,
it was a T-shaped garment, and the shoulders and sleeves
were not usually sewn, but fastened (the front to the back)
by small brooches as in the Ionic chiton.   The sleeves were
generally elbow length.   If the *stola* was cut without sleeves,
then there were sleeves on the *tunica interior*, which similarly
was sleeveless when the *stola* had sleeves.   The Roman
women had the armholes in the *sides* of their sleeveless
rectangular tunics, *not* on the *top edge*, which, it will be
remembered, was the favourite mode among the Greeks.
The *stola* reached to the feet and, if worn by a Roman matron,

had a narrow border (*instita*) at the bottom. It was girt under the breast. A special *stola*, worn as a sign of honour, had a gold border (*patagium*) at the hem.

The methods of draping the *palla* were infinitely varied. The method generally began, as in the simplest form of toga, by allowing the garment to hang forwards over the left shoulder to the feet, then passing it across the back towards the right. It might have a portion folded down from the upper edge as with the Greek himation, and might be drawn over the head or not as desired, and either over or under the right shoulder. It generally ended up by hanging over the left arm as did the toga. Sometimes it was wrapped tightly twice round the body, and the arms were often swathed in it even over the hands, *see* Fig. 122. The *palla* was, like the himation, of wool.

The Roman women, like the men, wore boots out of doors, and sandals in the house. The illustration, Fig. 127, is from the statue of a Roman priestess in the British Museum, and shows the *stola* without sleeves, the *tunica interior* showing elbow sleeves, and the *palla* used as a head-covering as well as a cloak.

ROMAN WOMEN'S HAIRDRESSING AND JEWELLERY

After the long ringlets of the Etruscan Era had been discarded we find, during the centuries more nearly preceding the Christian Era, the hair of the Roman women was on the whole very simply dressed ; but when we come to the Flavian or Hadrianic Period there is great elaboration and variety. Figs. 128a and c are from a bust said to be that of Julia, daughter of the Emperor Titus (*see* Fig. 99, dating A.D. 79–81). The immense curled frontage of this

coiffure must have been supported by a frame and the
minute plaiting of the knot at the back could have been
only accomplished by a skilled and patient worker devoting
unlimited time to getting the required effect.

By way of contrast to the somewhat frivolous type of
head shown at Figs. 128a and c we have in Fig. 128b a
portrait of the Abbess of the Vestal Virgins (" Virgo Vestalis
Maxima ") taken from a statue of the early second century
A.D. and now in the Museo delle Terme at Rome.   Her
ritual costume or uniform includes a woollen fillet with
pendant   bands   (infulae) ;   over   this   she   has   a   square
head-cloth with purple border (suffibulum)—this seems to
have been sewn up for a few inches in centre front, also
fastened with a brooch.   Her tunic (stola) and cloak (palla)
are like her head-fillet of wool and her woollen girdle is tied
in a special knot.   Fig. 128d is the loop attached to the top
of a golden " bulla," such as is worn by Fig. 124.   The
decoration here is an example of that type of jewellery
produced with such exquisite skill by the Etruscans.   It
consists in soldering on to the gold ground tiny grains of
gold (granaglia) to form patterns.   The grains vary in size
to suit the design but some are almost too small to be seen
with the naked eye.   The secret of making this wonderful
jewellery had been lost but a sufficiently successful attempt
was made to reproduce the methods in the late nineteenth
century by Count Castellane who found his workers, with
some tradition of the ancient skill still remaining, among
the Apennine Hills.   Fig. 128e is a betrothal ring and as
such needs no explanation.   There were numerous crowns
which symbolized achievement and gave distinction to their
wearers among the Romans ; of these, two have been selected
as examples.   Fig. 128h is the " Corona Muralis," a military

Fig. 128.

award, given for storming the walls of a city ; while Fig.
128*i* is the "Corona Navalis"—here the battlemented circlet
of Fig. 128*h* is exchanged for a circlet of pointed forms which
are intended to represent the prow of a ship. It was awarded
for the successful storming of a ship's deck. Most of the
dictionaries of Classical Antiquities give extensive information
on the subject of these Roman crowns and their symbolism.
Figs. 128*f* and *g* are examples of the elaborately decorated
high boot, similar to that worn by the Emperor Hadrian
when in his military costume, (*see* Fig. 111), while Figs.
128*j* and *l* show two of the many varieties of Roman
sandals. Fig. 128*k* represents the head-dress of a Roman

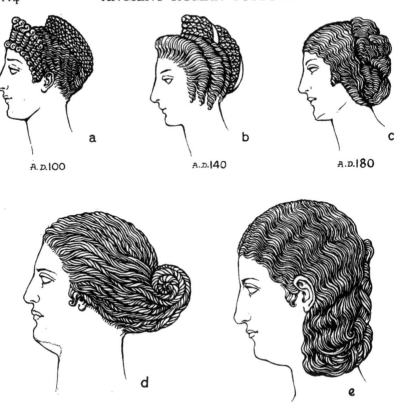

A.D. 100   A.D. 140   A.D. 180

Figs. 129*a* to 129*e*.

priest (*flamen*). A priest of the higher rank (*flamen diālis*) wore a pointed spike of olive wood (the " Apex ") set into the knob on the top of the helmet; those of inferior rank wore the helmet or cap without the spike. There is a group of priests wearing this helmet, shown in the processions from the Ara Pacis. The illustration Fig. 128*k* shows that the cap was tied with leather thongs under the chin. Apart from their characteristic head-dress the priests who form this procession are clad in the toga and *tunica* in similar fashion

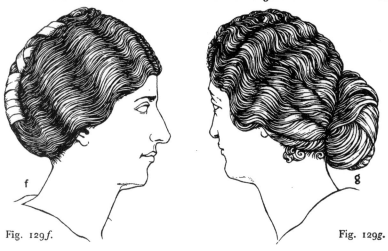

Fig. 129*f*.   Fig. 129*g*.

Fig. 129*h*.*

to their laymen fellow-citizens.

Though the costume of Roman women varied little, the styles in hairdressing showed constant change and variety. Figs. 129*a* to *h* illustrate several periods of hairdressing among Roman women of fashion in addition to those already shown at Figs. 128*a* and *c* and Fig. 128*b*. Figs. 129*a*, *b* and *c*, from busts in the British

* This drawing has been made, by permission, from a photograph, the property of Messrs. W. F. Mansell.

Museum, show great contrast and variety of style, continued in the examples given at Figs. 129*d* to *h*. Fig. 129*d* is from a bust of Antonia, wife of Drusus (period of Augustus, 31 B.C.–A.D. 14), whose sculptured portrait is also seen at Fig. 123 in the Ara Pacis procession, while Fig. 129*e*, represents Julia Donna, wife of the Emperor Septimius Severus (A.D. 193–211). Fig. 129*f* is a portrait of " Faustina the Elder," mother of Marcus Aurelius, and is of the Antonine Period; this bust is in the Louvre, Paris. Fig. 129*g* shows a lady of the court of the period of Marcus Aurelius (A.D. 161–180). These nine examples of hairdressing thus described give an idea of the enormous importance of coiffure in the otherwise very simple and almost unchangeable costume of the Roman lady during the first two centuries of the Christian Era. One more example, Fig. 129*h*, is from a portrait bust, now in the Vatican, of the famous queen of Palmyra, the heroic Zenobia, who, when defeated, was taken to Rome, where the Triumph of the Emperor Aurelian

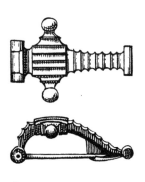

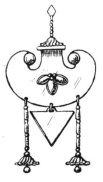

Late Roman Brooch. *Above :* Front view. *Below :* Side view. (*British Museum.*)

Etruscan Earring. (*Louvre, Paris.*)

Late Roman Brooch. Front view. (*British Museum.*)

Fig. 130.

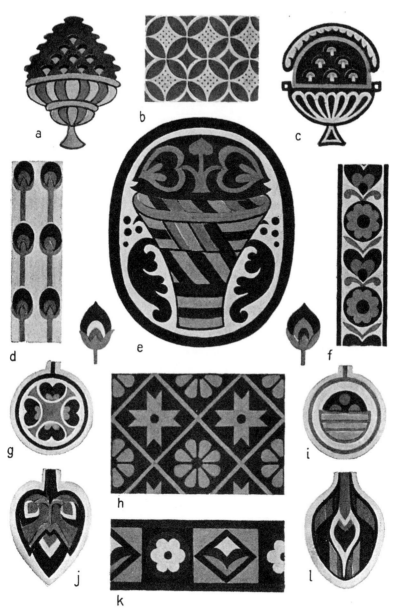

PLATE IV.—ROMAN ORNAMENT.

was graced by her presence (A.D. 274) when, we are told
" she walked laden with golden chains which others held."
This third-century bust shows the great queen dressed as a
Roman lady of fashion and indicates the influence of Rome
on court costume as far to the east as distant Palmyra.
Fig. 130 shows various examples of Etruscan and Roman
jewellery.

Roman Ornament

The themes of Roman architectural ornament and even
that applied to minor objects, such as bronze furniture, gold
and silver vessels and pottery, are probably well known to
everyone, comprising as they do the acanthus, palmette
and spiral of the Greeks. Indeed the two latter, palmette
and spiral, can be seen in familiar form upon the Roman
armour and even on the shoes in this volume (*see* Figs. 111,
118 and 128*k* and *g*.) Most of the ornament, however,
on dress materials and other woven fabrics was of a distinctly
different character. It is true that textiles were often
decorated with the same motifs that we find on buildings.
The human figure, the Greek acanthus scroll, the palmette
ornament occur, but their treatment by the textile designer
and weaver modifies their character so much that they seem
absolutely dissimilar. Where the technique of the sculptor
and metal worker permitted realistic effects, that of the
weaver made for stiffness and an almost primitive quaintness.
The textiles of Asia Minor and of Egypt supplied suggestions
to the Roman weaver and embroiderer which can be discerned in the examples in Plate IV., most of which are of
Egypto-Roman origin. Figs. *a*, etc., excepting *b* and *h*, are
all tapestry darned woollen embroideries from linen tunics
(and one from a coverlet in the British Museum). They

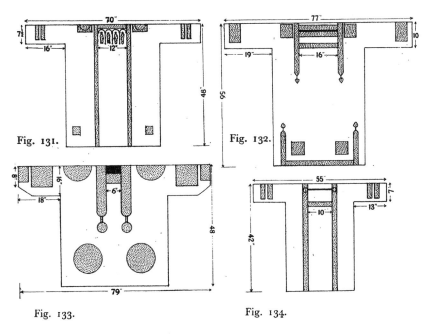

Fig. 131.   Fig. 132.

Fig. 133.   Fig. 134.

date round about the fourth to ninth century A.D. Fig. *b* is from an Egypto-Roman dye-printed fabric, and Fig. *h* is a woven silk pattern of a type produced in Hither Asia during the Roman Era.

Figs. 131 to 134, are drawings to scale and are from tunics in the Victoria and Albert Museum, contemporaneous with the ornament on Plate IV. and also of Egypto-Roman origin.

Fig. 135, the tailpiece to this chapter, represents a " Lar " or Household God. This little figure usually (as in the present case) takes the form of a dancing youth. It forms part of the panelled, high-relief decorations of an altar of the second century A.D. (now in the museum of the Palaggo dei Conservatori). The figure, here, has been chosen as an illustration on account of its charming costume where the girdle has a specially decorative effect. All of the classical dictionaries to which previous reference has been frequently made give extensive information on the " Lares et Penates," the Roman household gods, and their significance in Roman life.

Fig. 135.

CHAPTER IV

BYZANTINE COSTUME AND THE TRANSITION PERIOD TO WHICH IT IS THE SEQUEL

THE TRANSITION PERIOD STYLE IN COSTUME

Fig. 136.*

FROM the third century A.D. till the sixth century we see the gradual development from the Roman to the Byzantine style. In men's costume the increasing disuse of the toga (except when worn as a strictly official dress by the Emperor and afterwards also by the consuls) was the most notable change. The diagrams of the Romano-Egyptian tunics (Figs. 131 to 134) give an excellent idea of the *tunica* of this period. It shows an increased width compared with the tunics of earlier centuries both in body and sleeves. When the sleeves are of great width, measuring as much as ten inches or more across, we may cease to call the garment a *tunica* and regard it as a *dalmatic* (the name comes from Dalmatia,

* Fig. 136 is a motif in tapestry darning, carried out in purple, rose colour and green, and typical of late Roman dress decoration (British Museum).

120

Fig. 137a.

with whose inhabitants this roomy wide-sleeved garment
was a national dress). The decorations, Figs. 137a to d,
show in detail the ornaments which are disposed on the
ground of the tunics of this age and shown in mass without
details at Figs. 131 to 134. This type of decoration was
generally worked into the undyed wool or linen ground in
wools by the method known as " tapestry darning," i.e.
when the weft of the fabric is eliminated and its place taken
by a pattern darned in and out of the warp. These patterns
were chiefly worked in a dusky purple with touches of dull
blues, reds, greens and yellows as shown at Plate IV. The
dates of the ornaments at Figs. 137a to d have been given
as c. fourth to ninth century A.D., but similar patterns arranged to fill a square of from six inch to nine inch side persist

for several centuries after A.D. 800. Indeed, while the Victoria and Albert Museum, London, possesses a fine collection of fourth- to ninth-century tunics bearing this form of decoration, there is also a large display of tunics collected from the Greek islands and south-eastern Europe showing distinct traces of the traditions of fourth- to ninth-century modes, though the date of the more modern garments is for the most part of the late nineteenth or even of the present century.

Besides the actual garments (such as those at Figs. 131 to 134) which have been preserved to us, our sources of information for the costume of the Transition Period which bridges the gap between Roman and Byzantine costume are to be found chiefly among the following :

1. The " Consular Ivory Diptychs," now preserved in museums.
2. Fresco paintings in the Catacombs.
3. Sculpture from fourth century A.D. sarcophagi.
4. Mosaics from the earliest Christian churches.

To return to the toga which, as has been said, fell out of general use at this period, several illustrations of the Transition Period toga have been given on previous pages. The toga shown at Fig. 100, which is worn by a fourth-century magistrate, belongs to the Transition as also does that shown in the diagram at Fig. 103 (taken from the ivory diptych of the Consul Flavius Felix, A.D. 428). Again at Fig. 104 the method of draping a toga, dating A.D. 487, from the ivory diptych of the Consul Manlius Boethius is described in detail.

Finally, the ivory diptych of the Consul Anastasius,* A.D. 517, though really early sixth century, may be regarded as a very late example of a Roman consul's costume. He

* Now in Victoria and Albert Museum.

Fig. 137*b*.   Fig. 137*c*.   Fig. 137*d*.

wears a full-length long-sleeved *tunica talaris* with decorations
at wrists and hem, and bearing the two *clavi*. Over this is a
seven-eighths length *colobium* (which is cut wide enough to
fall to the elbows).* This was richly decorated all over its
surface. Above this wide *colobium* he wears the toga in its
last form, already referred to on pp. 92 as toga *picta*
and *contabulatum*, most richly decorated and worn folded.
The folds are only loosened for the last throw across the
front of the figure.

After this period the toga remained folded into a band
until the last throw across the front of the figure, and finally
the toga disappeared, leaving only the ornamental band
wrapped round the figure over two or more under-garments.†

* *See* pp. 125, 127.   † *See* Plate V*b*.

Fig. 138a is from the diptych itself and well illustrates the inability of the artists of this period to represent the human figure with any degree of realism. The panel (which is in the Victoria and Albert Museum, London) is a clumsy, though painstaking, attempt to represent Anastasius, seated in his chair and holding the symbols of consular authority in his hands—in his right hand is seen the *mappa* or napkin folded in a pad, which he used when giving the signals for the games to begin, while in his left he carries the ivory sceptre surmounted by an eagle as was also usual with consuls at the games of this period. In the original diptych the artist who executed the panel appears to have been much more concerned with the patterns which ornamented the various garments than with the correct representation of the drapery. In Fig. 138a the drawing gives rather more emphasis to the folds than will be found in the original ivory. In Figs. 138b and c, the garments were cut out draped upon a lay figure from which these two latter drawings have been sketched. It will be observed that the border of the toga in Figs. 138b and c is turned outwards throughout the draping for the sake of clearness, but in 138a this border is only visible on the vertical folds ; in those crossing the front of the figure in 138a the border is turned inwards and so does not show, yet the slightly different design of the ornament distinguishes the toga from the *colobium* beneath it.

The draping should be compared with those at Figs. 103 and 104. A very interesting ivory panel now at Monza Cathedral representing Pope Gregory the Great, " The Consul of God " (A.D. 590–604) shows him dressed in almost identical fashion with Fig. 138a save that the patterned *colobium* worn by Anastasius has been replaced by a similarly patterned

Fig. 138a.

dalmatic. The Victoria and Albert Museum has published excellent photographs of this diptych.

Fig. 138*d* shows border and all-over pattern of the toga of Anastasius; 138*e*, the all-over pattern of the wide *colobium*; 138*f*, the lower end of sleeve of the *tunica* worn under the *colobium*.

The frescoes from the Catacombs illustrate the introduction of the new style of dress prevailing in the third and fourth centuries A.D.

We find the men, who had by now discarded the toga for ordinary wear, dressed in a long-sleeved *tunica* worn to the ankle or knee length, according to rank and occupation. These tunics, as a rule, displayed the *clavi*. Over them the *paenula* or *pallium* might be worn as a wrap. A wide *colobium*, which also displayed the *clavi*, again of ankle or knee length, was popular, and, for dignified wear, over it was draped the *pallium*, after the simplest fashion of the Greek himation— namely, hanging over the left shoulder almost to the ankles or feet in front, slung across the back, under the right armpit, drawn across the front of waist and thrown over the bent left elbow (*see* Fig. 139). Almost all early representations of the apostles and saints are thus garbed in the wide *colobium* and *pallium* which were usually worn over a long tight-sleeved *tunica talaris*.

Fig. 139 is from the Catacombs and is considered to be that of an early Christian priest named Liberius. He wears over a long-sleeved *tunica* a *colobium* with the *clavi* and over that the *pallium* or cloak draped in the simplest manner which, as has been said, characterizes the representations of the apostles and saints of this era and survives even as late as the eleventh century for such sacred personages. This costume, as shown at Fig. 139, is similar to that worn

Fig. 138b.

Fig. 138c.

Fig. 138d.

Fig. 138f.

Fig. 138e.

by a sage or philosopher of the day. As yet, ecclesiastical costume, as such, can hardly be said to have existed in the Christian Church. This robe, or wide *colobium*, is identical in shape with a garment worn in Egypt and Persia centuries before the Christian Era, *see* refs. at Fig. 144*b*.

Fig. 140* (from the Catacombs) is the costume of a shepherd of the later fourth century in long-sleeved *tunica*, short *paenula*, with hood, and wearing a strapping of leather thongs from his ankle-boots to his knee. Fig. 141, also from the Catacombs, is an example of the *paenula*, decorated with *clavi* and worn over the *tunica*. Here we have the origin of the most important vestment of the Christian Church, namely the "chasuble" also shown in wear on the seventh-century representation of Pope

Fig. 139.

Symmachus *c.* 500 A.D., Fig. 154, and on Archbishop Maximianus at Fig. 149. In the case of Figs. 149 and 154 the chasuble is probably cut on the circular plan not the semicircular as at Fig. 141.

To return to the costume worn by Fig. 140 (that of the shepherd); it persisted as the dress of shepherds and agricultural workers in southern and western Europe as late as the thirteenth century except that the *clavi* and square patch of decoration were not present save in the Byzantine style. The *paenula* and hood for shepherds are seen in Mediaeval Manuscript Miniatures as late ·as the fifteenth century. It should be said, however, that the cross-gartering on the legs

* For method of cutting *paenula* on Figs. 140 and 141 refer to " burnous," Fig. 109, and join up front with a seam.

Fig. 140.

Fig. 141.

was not nearly so common as the high boot or stocking, usual in slightly varying forms in " peasant " costume of this era, and those which succeeded it. Compare Fig. 140 with the Roman shepherd at Fig. 108, Chapter III.

ARMOUR IN THE TRANSITION PERIOD

As the armour of the Transition shows little change from that of Imperial Rome, Figs. 142 and 143 will suffice to illustrate the military dress of this period. These two drawings are taken from a miniature entitled " Joshua and the Angel " in a manuscript of the fifth or sixth century which is now in the Vatican. Fig. 142, the Angel, is armed with a sword and Fig. 143 is that of Joshua who, besides his sword, carries, in addition, a spear.

The moulded cuirass edged with leather pendants worn by both figures is distinctively Roman as is also the military

cloak (*paludamentum*) and the high boots. The helmet of
Joshua, however, is not the typical close-fitting high-crested
Roman helmet such as leaders of distinction in the Roman
army wore. It resembles, in fact, much more nearly that
worn by the " Samnite " Gladiator at Fig. 115. A Carolingian manuscript " Bible of Charles the Bald " (Emperor
A.D. 875–877), now in Bibliothèque Nationale, Paris) shows
soldiers of the ninth century in Roman armour similar to
that of Fig. 143 and with somewhat similar helmets, which
are, however, surmounted by a ridge. (One of these head-
pieces is illustrated at Fig. 159 with further notes on the
armour.) Here we can imagine how the heroes of the
famous Emperor Charlemagne were armed when Roland
blew his horn at Roncesvalles—and indeed this panoply
might more truly represent the armour of Arthur of Britain
and his knights than those mediaeval trappings with which
the mind of Sir Thomas Malory invested them. Again it
is interesting to compare the helmet of Fig. 143 with the
sixteenth-century *salade* or *sallet*. In Meyrick's book
on " Antient Armour " there is illustrated an " Italian
Archer's salade, with comb. (Lucca), A.D. 1540 " and again
a " Salade with occularium used until the commencement
of the sixteenth century " both of which have points of
resemblance to the helmets of the Gladiator at Fig. 115,
Chapter II., of Joshua at Fig. 143 and also that shown at
Fig. 159. This is somewhat remarkable when the very
different head-pieces of the thirteenth, fourteenth and
fifteenth centuries which intervened are considered.

WOMEN'S DRESS IN THE TRANSITION PERIOD

While the *palla* and *stola* are still seen in the representations of women's costume after the third century A.D.

Fig. 142.   Fig. 143.

we find the *stola* gradually disappears, its place being taken
by that wide robe (*colobium*) which became popular for
both men's and women's dress about this time and which
was generally worn over a long-sleeved inner tunic in contrast to the elbow-sleeved inner garment which we see in
wear at Figs. 126 and 127. This robe or *colobium*, it must
be remembered, was in common wear both in Asia and
Egypt many centuries previously. We see it, for example,
worn by Darius, King of Persia fifth and sixth centuries B.C.
(the Median " Robe of Honour ") and again on the Pharoah
in Egypt as early as 1400 B.C. Fig. 144*b* is taken from a
fifth-century ivory diptych now in the treasury of Monza

Cathedral—where the male figure Fig. 144a, is said by some authorities to be that of Stilicho ("the Vandal") the commander-in-chief of the Imperial Army, while others consider it to be that of his successor, Aetius ("the last of the Romans"). The woman at Fig. 144b, is generally identified as Galla Placidia, Empress Regent for her small son, the future Emperor Valentinian III. who, in the original diptych, stands beside his mother and is dressed in similar manner to the male figure at 144a. It will be observed that Fig. 144b, has her robe fringed up the side seam on the left. This probably indicates that there is no seam on the right side but instead the material would be folded over and there would be a seam upon each shoulder leaving an aperture for the neck, also an aperture would be cut in the material to admit the right arm and a similar space arranged at the top of the fringed seam on the left. This garment was probably woven specially to the correct size as was the common practice in ancient times. The *palla* worn by this figure is unusually small. The head-dress shows strong Asiatic influences. The jewelled belt, ear-rings and necklace are all of a much more massive type than those worn by the ancient Greeks and Romans. This costume, excepting the head-dress, may be said to be highly representative of its period and it persists in the representations of female saints and sacred personages as late as the eleventh century. To return to the man's costume, Fig. 144a, his semi-military dress includes a knee-length tight-sleeved tunic and the *paluda-mentum* which is here fastened with a brooch or pin on the right shoulder. Both cloak and tunic are richly decorated all over with what is most probably a tapestry-darned pattern. The cloak has a design of circles filled with human busts (Fig. 144c) while the tunic is decorated with a pattern,

Fig. 144a.   Figs. 144c and d.   Fig. 144b.

having similar circles but, in addition, arcades filled with
full-length human figures (Fig. 144d). The wall paintings
of the Catacombs at Rome are an important source of
information as to the costumes of the early Christians.
Three have been already shown at Figs. 139, 140 and 141—
the dates of the Catacomb costumes extend from the second
century A.D. until the fifth (the Catacombs were closed A.D.
410); during this period there is little change in the style, but
certain portraits of the dead represented in an attitude of
prayer (" Orantes ") illustrate most clearly the popularity
of an early type of *dalmatic*. Figs. 145, 146 and 147 show three
Roman ladies in the attitude of prayer, which enables one
to see very clearly how their garments were cut, and each

one is different from the other but on a similar plan. The
method of hairdressing shows a complete change of style
from most of those shown in Chapter II., though the head at
Fig. 129c which is dated A.D. 180 has a similar heavy low-
placed coiffure tending towards the later fashions at Figs.
145 to 147.

THE BYZANTINE STYLE IN COSTUME

Though true Byzantinism is said to date from the reign
of the Emperor Leo III. (" The Isaurian "), A.D. 717–741, the
costumes here described date from the sixth century A.D.
till the end of the twelfth century, and in addition a few
examples of the thirteenth century are given. Those illustrated are for the most part of Court dress. We gain our
knowledge of the period chiefly from mosaic wall-decorations
in churches, ivory carvings and illuminated manuscripts.
When the Roman Emperor Constantine in A.D. 324 removed
the seat of his government to Byzantium (renaming it Constantinople) it naturally followed that his capital city became
the great centre of culture in Europe. Its position, so closely
adjacent to Asia, was favourable for the import of the silken
stuffs and jewels of the East—in effect, everything combined
to produce a style of costume surpassingly rich and splendid.
Gold and precious stones were freely used in the decoration
of garments. We read, for example, of Maria, daughter of
Stilicho, and wedded to the Emperor Honorius, that when
her grave was opened in 1544 her golden shroud was melted
down and yielded 36 lb. of pure gold. Such weaving with
flattened strips of pure gold was still in vogue as late as the
beginning of the tenth century. While the garments such as
those of the Consul Anastasius at Fig. 138a are of a rich and
splendid type, the costume of the Byzantine style becomes

Fig. 145.   Fig. 146.   Fig. 147.

each century more sumptuous, until the late examples from
the tenth to the thirteenth century are of surpassing magnificence, yet, owing to the simplicity of their construction,
dignified in the extreme.

All through the period, in spite of its gorgeous decorations,
the style retains the simple T-shaped tunic of primitive cut,
merely varying its length, width and proportion of its sleeves ;
also the outer garments are still rectangular, semi-circular
or circular cloaks. The dresses worn by the Byzantine Court
and nobility influenced those of practically all the other
Courts of Europe. We can trace the style through Germany
and France to far-away England, and in Russia the Byzantine
style dominated the ceremonial costumes of the Court until
its recent downfall in the twentieth century.

Previous to the sixth century the cultivation of the
silkworm was unknown in Europe. It was owing to its

introduction from Persia during the reign of Justinian that silk-weaving gained an enormous impetus under the patronage of the Emperor, and hence the magnificence of costume increased.

The style of dress worn in the sixth and seventh centuries did not materially differ from that of the fifth. The examples from a sixth-century mosaic are those of the Emperor Justinian and his wife, Theodora, in the church of S. Vitali, Ravenna, Figs. 148a and b. Justinian wears a knee-length tunic in white with embroidered decorations in gold, his legs are covered by tights (hosa) in purple, his red shoes are decorated with pearls. His cloak, purple lined with red, is semi-circular, not rectangular, though still given the name *paludamentum*. This *paludamentum* shows the embroidered panel (called the *tablion*) which was an important feature of men's Court dress from the fifth to the tenth century, and even later. On it was lavished the most sumptuous decoration of the whole costume. As a rule, it was of cloth of gold embroidered in jewels. The Empresses wore it also from the eighth to the eleventh century, but otherwise it was confined to the Emperor and his nobles. The Empress Theodora has an Oriental head-dressing of similar type to that of Galla Placidiat (Fig. 144b) beneath her crown. Her white, gold-embroidered tunic is similar to the Emperor's, save in its length. Her blue-lined purple cloak is semi-circular, and the golden embroidery at its hem has for its subject the adoration of the Magi. The latter are represented in Asiatic (Phrygian) costume, as was usual at this period. The jewelled collar (*superhumeral*) on the shoulders recalls ancient Egyptian models.

The gentlemen of the Court (*see* Fig. 152) are dressed in a less richly decorated form of the dress of Justinian, and are

A   B

C   D   E

Fig. 148.

bare-headed. The Court ladies are again similarly dressed
to the Empress in long tunics and cloaks. Those four ladies
whose garments are most clearly indicated show a delightful
variety of pattern, both in form and colour. The lady nearest
Theodora (*see* Fig. 151) wears a reddish purple robe or *dalmatic*, with all-over geometric pattern in black (Fig. 148e) ;
it is decorated with two golden stripes (*clavi*), having an
embroidered pattern of rosebuds in natural colours. Her
cloak is of cream and green, with touches of red. Her head-
dressing is in the turban-like fashion of the time. The second
lady has a cream robe, with a pattern of blue ducks and
black spots (Fig. 148d) ; her cloak is in gold, with red roses
and green leaves (Fig. 148c), and her hairdressing is similar
to that of the first lady.

Fig. 149 is that of the Archbishop Maximianus. He
wears over a *tunica* with tight wrist-length sleeves the *dalmatic*
which has itself developed longer sleeves and resembles in
cut that vestment known in the fifteenth century as the
surplice; the *dalmatic* still carries the *clavi* and has two narrow
stripes on the sleeves as well. Over the *dalmatic* we see the
chasuble and again over that there is passed round his shoulders
the *ecclesiastical pallium* now shown in wear in this volume
for the first time. Quoting here from Planché* we have the
following explanation : " This word (*pallium*), which among
the Romans signified a cloak was applied in the eighth
century to a long band of white linen (afterwards in the
Western Church of lamb's wool) about 3 fingers wide, which
encircled the shoulders, the two extremities hanging down
before and behind as low as the bottom of the *chasuble*. It
formed the distinctive ornament of an Archbishop." Compared with Fig. 154 the seventh-century vestments are identical

* Encyclopaedia of Costume.

Fig. 149.　　　Fig. 150.　　　Fig. 151.　　　Fig. 152.　　　Fig. 153.

and this Fig. 154 (*see* p. 141) is that of Pope Symmachus (*c.* A.D. 500) as represented standing beside S. Agnese (Plate V.). Compare these simple flowing garments with those of Fig. 155 where we see an eleventh-century representation of St. Clement vested in *dalmatic*, characteristic eleventh-century form of the *chasuble* and the fully-shaped *pallium* of the Western Church. . "The *pallium* should be embroidered with four crosses before and behind but the number was sometimes exceeded." This quotation from Planché refers to the Mediaeval Period, when the whole system of the vestments of the Western Church had been permanently fixed and which with a few minor changes, such as the alteration in shape of the sides of the *chasuble*, remains in force at present. It will be noticed that the (ecclesiastical) *pallium* of this archbishop, Fig. 154, is shorter than the prescribed length and displays only one cross. This archi-episcopal costume belongs, of course, to the period before the division of the Church into that of the East and West. In the Western Church, it should be said, the *pallium* is now only granted by the Pope. This description has been given at some length as this word *pallium* with its entirely different implications is a source of great confusion to the student of costume when not thoroughly understood. Quoting from Smith's *Dictionary of Greek and Roman Antiquities* we find it says "Pallium (Palla, *see* Pallium) diminutive Palliolum, Plural Pallia. A rectangular piece of cloth nearly square. The Pallium was used as a counterpane at night also for carpets and the sails of ships, lastly the *pallium* with the *tunica*. The *sagum* of the Northern nations was a woollen *pallium* fastened like that of the Greeks by a brooch or thorn. Under the Roman republic and the early emperors the *toga* was worn by men instead of the *pallium* who considered that to be ' palliatus ' or ' sagatus '

Fig. 154.   Fig. 155.

instead of 'togatus' indicated an affectation of Greek or even of barbarian manners."

To turn back to Fig. 150, we see here an ecclesiastic beside the archbishop; he wears the *dalmatic* and it is clear he has the tonsure. In Chapter V. the distinctive vestments of the Eastern Orthodox Church (after the Great Schism) are illustrated and fully described with their proper Greek nomenclature.

Fig. 153 is one of the Emperor's bodyguard. His tunic is decorated after the manner of those shown at Figs. 131 to 134. Round his neck he wears the jewelled collar of his order and his shield bears the sacred monogram in jewelled lettering.

This emblem is called the " Chi Rho " a phonetic rendering of the two Greek letters " X " and " P " corresponding in English to our letters Ch.* and R.   In the Greek language XP are the first two letters of the sacred name ΧΡΙΣΤΟΣ (CHRISTOS).   For Figs. 154 and 155 *see* p. 141.

The seventh and eighth centuries, owing to the Mohammedan invasions, were not so favourable to the development of the arts, including that of costume, as the previous and succeeding periods.   Much of the art production of this time must necessarily have been destroyed ; nevertheless we have sufficient evidence to show that no great change, but rather a slow development, took place.   Before leaving the sixth-century style we may note two costumes from a mosaic in the Church of S. Apollinare Nuovo at Ravenna.

The mosaic has for its subject a procession of twenty-two virgin martyrs offering their crowns to the Blessed Virgin and is complementary to the procession opposite from which Fig. 157 is taken.   These virgin martyrs wear (as at Fig. 156) a style of Court dress which is characteristic of the wrapped-round draperies of the *palla,* so much favoured by the Roman ladies (*see* Figs. 122, 123, Chapter III.) and which, at the same time, displays the lavish ornament beloved by the Byzantines.   The artists who executed these processional figures were chiefly concerned with the decorative effect as a whole and not with the exact representation of either the human form or of draperies at which indeed at this period they did not excel (compare Fig. 138a for this inability to represent).

While the artist's intention, therefore, is not made quite clear the costume of Fig. 156 and her twenty-one companions may be explained as follows.   Over a long tunic (*stola*) of

* Ch. here pronounced as in the Scottish word " loch."

Fig. 156.

which only the jewelled cuffs are visible, we see the *colobium* which in Fig. 156 is without decoration, but which in the other twenty-one figures shows the characteristic *clavi* or stripes usually in the form of two floral bands (for these *clavi*, compare with Fig. 151); over this is draped an embroidered and jewelled *palla* measuring probably about one yard wide by some five yards long. It may be taken that the square-ended jewelled panel seen hanging down almost to the feet in front is the end of the *palla* folded after the manner of a Roman Consul's toga (*see* Figs. 138*b* and *c*). This jewelled panel forming a wide border along one side of the *palla* does not show elsewhere. The garment thus folded is passed upwards and under a cord tied round the waist, then spread out and thrown back over the left shoulder (it seems to be lined with white and here this lining shows as a narrow white strip passing from waist at right upwards towards left shoulder). Passing round the back it is slipped under her waist-belt rather after the method seen at Fig. 138*c*. The *palla* is then drawn over the right shoulder, slipped across the front of breast and under the left shoulder draping round towards the back, where it is allowed to fall over the lower limbs; it is then draped round the right thigh almost at full width. Last of all it is drawn upwards across the limbs in front, forming an oblique line and some folds are tucked into the waist-belt at the left side. The remainder of the *palla* can be drawn round under the waist-belt to the centre back of waist and then allowed to hang down, where, if sufficiently long, it forms a kind of train. It is interesting to compare Fig. 156 with two other representations of this style of dress (not here illustrated) which show the costume in full front view. One is a representation of the Blessed Virgin as a Byzantine Queen, now at St. Mark's, Florence, and dating from the beginning of the eighth century, and the other is a representation of St. Agnes from the Church of S. Prassede, Rome, the mosaic here dating *c.* A.D. 825 The jewelled belt and wide jewelled collar of Fig. 156 are put on after the draping of the *palla* has been completed. The line crossing the *palla* in front from right knee to left hip, may be a species of girdle for the draping, perhaps a metal chain. In the case of St. Agnes at S. Prassede the drapery certainly seems to hang over it at the right side as if supported or caught up, but again the lack of exact representation of the drapery makes this uncertain.

Fig. 157, that of a martyred saint* offering his crown to the Redeemer is simply robed in a *dalmatic* with the *clavi* and over it a semi-circular cloak shaped like that of Figs. 148*a* and *b*, but draped equally over each shoulder and having the right corner tucked into a waist-belt or perhaps merely kept in place by pressure of the left elbow against the side. An interesting illustration is that of a figure of St. Agnes (Plate V.*B*), as she stands between the two popes, Honorius and Symmachus, from a mosaic in her Basilica at Rome, which belongs to the first half of the seventh century. The saint is dressed in the costume of a seventh-century Empress. Her inner garment is a tight-sleeved tunic ; over

* From the same mosaic as Fig. 156.

PLATE V.—BYZANTINE COSTUME.

A. A Princess of the Western Empire,
from a 10th century textile
Bamberg Cathedral.

B. St Agnes in the dress of a Byzantine Empress, from a 7th century
mosaic in her Basilica at Rome.

it a *dalmatic* or possibly a *colobium*, (the indication at the sleeves is not very clear), with three-quarter length sleeves, decorated with jewelled stripes (*clavi*) and embroidered motifs (*segmentae*) placed just below the knees. Over her *dalmatic* she wears a long jewelled band, which is in reality a survival of the embroidered border of the latest form of the folded toga. The omophorion or wide decorated band worn by bishops of the Eastern Orthodox Church at Liturgical Services is almost identical with the band seen on this costume. It is also similar to the ecclesiastical *pallium* as at Fig. 149 but much wider and richly jewelled ; compare also with Fig. 156. It was worn over both shoulders, end hanging to front and back as indicated in the drawing, and was at first

Fig. 157.

fastened by pins. The belt which here keeps it in place is an unusual arrangement. We may date the development of ecclesiastical costume from the sixth century. The long tight-sleeved tunic became the *albe*, the outer tunic with shorter and wider sleeves the *dalmatic*, and was the special garment of deacons ; the *paenula* became the *cope, cappa* or *pluviale*, and, as the last name implies, was originally for outdoor use as a protection from rain.

Fig. 154, Pope Symmachus (*c.* A.D. 500), *see* p. 141, is taken from the same seventh-century mosaic as that of St. Agnes. We see here the *chasuble* in an early form, apparently cut on a fully circular plan and long enough to touch the ground. Compare with Fig. 149.

Byzantine soldiers retained the Roman military costume for centuries. As late as the twelfth century we find the moulded metal or metal-scaled cuirass (*lorica*), with the leather strips fringing it at armholes and hips. The tunic is longer and the helmet more of the shape of the late fifteenth-century salade, otherwise there is little difference between the twelfth-century Byzantine soldier shown at Fig. 158 and that of Imperial Rome. But by the eleventh century the influences from Hither Asia and north-west Europe had obliterated much of the Romano-Byzantine style in armour, and the introduction of chain-mail with the conical steel cap instead of the ancient helmet produced a style which began to approximate to the familiar mail-clad knight of the early Middle Ages.

Fig. 158 is from a twelfth-century sculpture presenting St. George. The cuirass and cloak are still those of ancient Rome. The greaves are a somewhat unusual feature. He wears no helmet but it would be most probably of the type of Fig. 159, which is from a ninth-century Carolingian manuscript.* The soldier who wears this helmet has also the Roman cuirass and cloak and his feet are shod with high laced boots which leave the toes bare as at Fig. 116 in Chap. III. The dress of the common folk was fairly constant in type from the fourth century till the twelfth century. The changes which took place in the dress of a man of the working class (as typified by the shepherd at Fig. 140) were, first, the substitution of a short rectangular or semi-circular cloak fastened on the right shoulder in place of the *paenula* ; secondly, the disappearance of the *clavi* and *segmentae* from the tunic, and in

* *The Bible of Charles the Bald*, Bibliothèque Nationale, Paris.

the case of well-to-do citizens, the addition of bands of decoration at the neck, round the arms and at the hem instead. The legs were no longer left uncovered, stockings (*hosa*) were worn, and over them occasionally boots reaching to the calf. The cross-garterings as worn by the shepherd were also worn over the stockings, and also over the looser breeches of Frankish origin which were sometimes seen. To cover the head was the rule. Round flat-topped caps and later conical caps of Phrygian type were in use. The working woman was clad in two tunics and a cloak, as in the Roman Era. The inner long-sleeved tunic was constant in shape, but the outer gradually changed from the wide sleeveless

Fig. 159.

Fig. 158.

robe of the fifth centuries to the tighter short-sleeved *dalmatic* of the seventh and eighth centuries, and eventually was made to fit the body and upper arm more closely, while the skirt portion and lower-arm part of sleeve hung full and long. The women's semi-circular cloaks after the sixth century were worn in symmetric fashion, often thrown over the head and, if fastened, were clasped with a brooch in the centre of the breast. The representations of the Blessed Virgin dressed as an ordinary woman of the working class show the *palla* or rectangular cloak still in use as late as the twelfth century. *See* Fig. 160, which is taken from a mosaic in the Church of La Martorana, Palermo, *c.* A.D. 1143. She is clad in a Roman *stola* only, but with long sleeves, and over it the *palla*, which has been arranged with an over-fold after the manner of the Doric *chiton*. The garment is then hung round the shoulders evenly, with the ends hanging down in front over each shoulder. The over-fold is then lifted up at the back of the neck and used as a hood ; also the right corner of the over-fold in front is thrown across the chest and backwards over the left shoulder ; this wraps up the figure thoroughly and protects from cold. The fringes decorating this *palla* would not, of course, be worn by a working-class woman. They are probably attached to each end of the *palla* leaving the sides plain but they are not indicated by the twelfth-century artist with any exactitude.

Fig. 161 is taken from a manuscript in the Vatican, dating tenth or eleventh century. The figure is entitled " Wisdom," and is an example of the simpler older style of dress being used by artists when representing sacred or symbolic per- sonages. Here we have the *tunica* and *colobium* as on the figure of Galla Placidia at Fig. 144*b*. The small *palla* (almost a scarf) worn by Galla Placidia is in contrast to the heavy voluminous one which is seen at Fig. 161.

The foundation of the Holy Roman Empire of the West under Charlemagne in the year A.D. 800 and the Emperor's patronage of the arts, more especially his feeling for the dignity and beauty of imperial dress, were responsible for increasing the dissemination of Byzantine fashions in the Courts of western Europe. We have a detailed description of the State dress of Charlemagne ; there are also some fragments which are considered to be part of his vestments and which are still in existence, though the garments he is depicted as wearing in the very carefully detailed picture of him painted

Fig. 160.   Fig. 161.

by Albrecht Dürer in the sixteenth century are now considered to be of twelfth-century origin, and will be better
described and enumerated under that date.

An interesting development of fashion during the tenth
century in Byzantine women's dress was the short over-tunic,
either with sleeves or without.   The example on Plate V.*A*
(*left*) is from a tenth-century textile from the tomb of Bishop
Gunther in Bamberg Cathedral, and represents, symbolically,

a princess of the Western Empire proffering homage to the
Byzantine Emperor (Nicephorus Phocas). Her garments
are all cut upon the simple straight-lined plan, typical of the
Byzantine style. Her long tight-sleeved tunic is richly
decorated with jewelled bands. Her sleeveless over-tunic
curiously forestalls the fashion of the mediaeval surcoat. Her
belt of ceremony has two pendentives of identical shape with
those on the shoulders of the men's tunics of the sixth century.
Her *palla* is so small as to be a mere scarf, and her hair in its
loose freedom shows an entirely new style of dressing.

A very magnificent pair of Court costumes are those of
Romanus and Eudocia, Figs. 162*a* and 162*b*, rulers at
Constantinople in A.D. 1068–1071 They are portrayed on
a carved ivory panel of the period, now in the Bibliothèque
Nationale, Paris.* Romanus, Fig. 162*a*, wears the long
tight-sleeved under-tunic, over this a long *dalmatic* with
the *clavi* and *segmentae* in jewelled embroidery. Over the
dalmatic we see the *pallium* as worn by the laity in its new
form, namely, as a long strip (in this case a very wide one)
with a hole for the head and ends hanging down front
and back; indeed this lay *pallium* now resembles the
scapular worn by so many of the Religious Orders
during the Middle Ages, as, for example, in the habit of the
Dominicans. The back end in this costume is long enough
to trail on the ground, and is shown drawn across the front
of body and hung over the left arm. The *pallium* is entirely
covered with richly jewelled embroidery and would be most
probably of cloth of gold. Eudocia, Fig. 162*b*, is clad in the
tight-sleeved under-tunic, and *dalmatic* similar to that of
Romanus ; it is decorated with plaques and bands of
jewelled embroidery and is confined at the waist with
a girdle. Her richly decorated *paludamentum* is of the

* There is an excellent cast of this ivory in the Victoria and Albert Museum.

Fig. 162*a*.   Fig. 162*b*.

semi-circular type with a curve cut out to allow of flatter fitting round the neck, and it bears the *tablion*, which among women the Empress alone was entitled to wear.

For shape of *paludamentum see* Fig. 163*a*.

Plate VI. is from a Greek manuscript of the eleventh century, now in the Bibliothèque Nationale in Paris. It represents the Byzantine Emperor Nicephorus Botaniates, A.D. 1078–1081. Nothing could well give a better idea of the magnificence of the dress of the period. The simply cut garments have all been previously described as to their shaping ; his tight-sleeved purple under-tunic shows embroidery of golden scroll-work at the wrists, and the hem is enriched by a band in cloth of gold, embroidered in silver scrollwork sewn with pearls. The purple and gold silk *dalmatic* is split up the front almost as far as the knees ; also two small *segmentae*, formerly placed below the knees, are now much higher up, and on the arms their place is taken by a band. The deep collar (*superhumeral*) has developed a pendant in front which has retained the heart-shaped

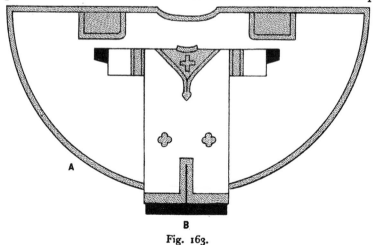

Fig. 163.

ending characteristic of some of the
embroidered shoulder bands of the
fourth to sixth century. The diagram
163*b*, opposite, indicates the simple cut
of *tunica* and *dalmatic*. Fig. 163*a* shows
the cutting of a *paludamentum* as worn
by this Emperor in another portrait ;
it is of blue silk or velvet, the pattern
of which is seen at *b* on Plate
VII.,* where other details from the
costume shown in Plate VI. have
also been enlarged, and will easily
be recognized.

It should be noted that the *tablion*
or rectangular panel decorating the
paludamentum, Fig. 163*a*, always occurs
at both sides of the garment, *i.e.* the
front and the back.

Fig. 164 is a representation of the
Empress Maria, Queen of Nicephorus
Botaniates. This costume has points
of resemblance to that of the Emperor
Romanus (Fig. 162*a*) and also that of
(Fig. 166) the Emperor Andronicus

Fig. 164.

Palaeologus. Over the inner *stola* or tunic she wears a
dalmatic of richly patterned silk reaching to the feet, and
with sleeves which, narrow at the top, are of great width at
the wrist and are lined with plain material. Round the
upper arm and at the hem are bands of heavy gold embroidery showing the favourite Byzantine scroll-work pattern.
The (lay or non-ecclesiastical) *pallium* like that worn by Figs.
162*a* and 166 is long enough to form a train at the back and

* See inside back cover for color version.

is held up in front showing that it has, in this case, a semi-circular end. This costume very much resembles the historic dress worn on occasions at the Russian Court by the Empresses up till the period of the Revolution. Fig. 164 is from a manuscript, " Homilies of St. John Chrysostom," in the Bibliothèque Nationale, Paris. In this miniature the Empress is seen beside the Emperor but here his costume is not shown in such detail as that representing him on Plate VI. where in

Fig. 165.

the original manuscript he is represented as standing between St. John Chrysostom who wears the *tunica, colobium* and circular *chasuble* (as at Fig. 149) while on the Emperor's other side is the Archangel Michael clad in *tunica, colobium* and military *paludamentum* with the *tablion* (as at Fig. 152). Fig. 165 represents the Emperor Basil II. (A.D. 958–1025) from a contemporary manuscript. His costume illustrates the imperial military dress of the period and there are still traces of the Roman influence apparent in his scaled c u i r a s s (*squamata*) military *paludamentum* and under-tunic. He wears *hosa* or stockings however, unlike the Romans, as are also his high boots, sewn with pearls, which are probably borrowed from Asiatic sources.

PLATE VI.—BYZANTINE COSTUME.

The Emperor Nicephorus Botaniates (11th century), from a manuscript in the
Bibliothèque Nationale, Paris.

Fig. 166.

Fig. 166 represents the Byzantine Emperor Andronicus Palaeologus, showing the imperial dress of the late thirteenth century. It has points of resemblance to that of the eleventh-century imperial costumes already described. The garments worn are a long, tight-sleeved *tunica*, a long *dalmatic* with seven-eighth length sleeves, and slit up in front as in the case of Nicephorus (Plate VI.), an embroidered and jewelled *superhumeral* and last of all, a late form of the " lay " *pallium* narrower than that worn by Romanus, (Fig. 162*a*), and having the top part formed by four straps, two over the shoulders and two round the top of each arm. The crown is completely altered, and has a distinctly Oriental character.

Reference has been made to the influence of Byzantine fashions on the costumes of the Western or Holy Roman Empire, after its foundation in the year A.D. 800 by the Emperor Charlemagne. From this period until the thirteenth century the Byzantine style dominated the Court costumes of Germany and France, and, to some extent, of England. A German ruler of the eleventh or twelfth century (Fig. 167*a*), when in full imperial dress, was clad as follows : A full-length tunic (*tunicella*), shaped as in the diagram, Fig. 167*b*, of deep purple silk embroidered in gold and pearls, and with

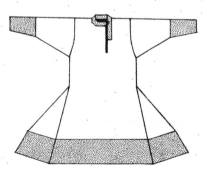

Fig. 167*b*.

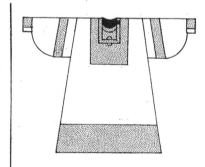

Fig. 167*c*.

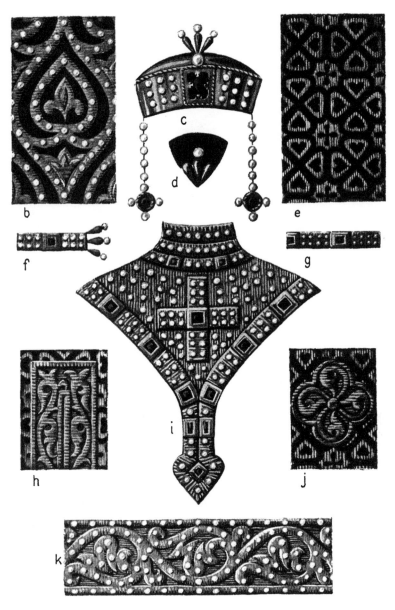

PLATE VII.—DETAILS OF BYZANTINE COSTUME.

(See inside back cover for color version.)

Fig. 167a.

a wide hem of red also embroidered in gold. Over the *tunicella* was worn the *alba camisia*, cut as shown in the diagram, Fig. 167c ; it was of white silk and decorated with purple bands on the sleeves and a wide purple hem.   Plate VIII. illustrates the pattern decorating the *alba* ;   this detail is from one of the sleeve-bands, and is of Oriental design, richly embroidered in gold and pearls.   Over the *alba camisia* there was a band (*stola*, formerly *pallium*), about nine inches wide and richly embroidered and jewelled.   It was worn as shown, Fig. 167a, and kept in position by a girdle. The details in the diagram, Fig. 167a, have been much simplified for the sake of clearness of illustration.   [We should here again note that a certain confusion is caused by the change in meaning of the word *stola* (English stole), formerly describing the Roman woman's tunic, and now applied to the wide band hitherto and still described as the *pallium*.   This confusion of terms is an unfortunate feature of the nomenclature of costume in many instances, so that close reference to

Fig. 167d.

Fig. 167e.

PLATE VIII.—DETAIL FROM BYZANTINE COSTUME.

Fig. 167f.

Fig. 167g.

diagrams and drawings is constantly necessary.] A cope (*paludamentum imperialis*) was worn over all. For cutting out cope *see* Fig. 163a, p. 152.

The crown worn with this costume was made of eight plates of gold hinged together and enriched with enamels and precious stones. A cross· was placed over the centre front plate and a bridge or arch joined back to front, as shown in Fig. 167d ; the orb is shown at Fig. 167e, the gloves and shoes at Figs. 167f and 167g.

The costumes already illustrated in this chapter have given in considerable detail the types of design used in Byzantine embroidered and jewelled dress decorations. The woven patterns of the silk materials of the period are of such surpassing grandeur and beauty that they are worthy of careful study. The favourite pattern was based on the roundel, and is of Sassanian Persian origin ; the subjects enclosed by the roundels were frequently human figures

Fig. 168.

hunting wild beasts surrounded by a decorated band, but
animals and birds either alone or facing each other were,
perhaps, the most popular of all.   When in the twelfth
century, at the cathedral of Aix-la-Chapelle, the tomb of
Charlemagne was opened, and the Emperor discovered
sitting on his ivory throne, some fragments of his imperial
vestments were still intact.

A finely designed specimen of the roundel type from
the Berlin Museum has been identified with the Emperor by
some authorities, while others declare it to be of the tenth
century and placed in the tomb when it was opened about
this period.   It consists of roundels, each enclosing a single

elephant, indicated with the splendid vigour and decorative feeling for which the Sassanian style, and the styles derived from it, were famed. This particular specimen is of

Fig. 170.

a derivative style, having been woven at Constantinople (*see* Fig. 168).

The textiles, Figs. 169 and 170, are of Flemish manufacture in gold, linen and wool, dating thirteenth century, and illustrate the widespread and persistent influence of the Byzantine style on pattern weaving even at this comparatively late period. The details are simple and somewhat crude compared to those of Sassanian and Byzantine manufacture.

Fig. 169.

CHAPTER V

THE VESTMENTS OF THE EASTERN ORTHODOX CHURCH AND THEIR RELATION TO BYZANTINE COSTUME

THE examples chosen to illustrate this chapter are taken chiefly from the Greek and Russian branches of the Eastern Church and date from the ninth century A.D. until modern times.

In Chapter IV. ecclesiastical costume of the earlier Byzantine period is given, as at Figs. 139, 149, 150 and 154, but these early types may be considered equally as the basis of the vestments of the Western Church.

It is from the drawings shown in Chapter V. that we can see the distinctive differences between East and West.

Figs. 171, 172 and 173, are those of two Patriarchs (171, 173) and a Bishop (172) of the Greek Church. All three are of ninth-century date. The two Patriarchs are from paintings at Mount Athos Monastery, while the Bishop is from a ninth-century MS. (A.D. 886). In these three sets of vestments the style is seen developing, but not yet fully formed, and before describing Figs. 171, 172 and 173 in more detail it will be desirable to enumerate the chief vestments worn by the ecclesiastics of a later date when the separation of the Eastern and Western Churches emphasized the differences of the ceremonial garments pertaining to each.

The following vestments here enumerated are those in

Fig. 171.   Fig. 172.   Fig. 173.

use by the Greek branch of the Eastern Church and are
almost identical with those used by the Russian branch in
modern times.

The Vestments

1. The Sticharion (A, that
   of the Priest, B, that
   of the Deacon).
2. The Epitrachelion.
3. The Zone.
4. The Sakkos.
5. The Epigonation.

6. The Omophorion
   (Great and Lesser).
7. The Epimanikia.
8. The Phenolion.
9. The Orarion.
10. The Mitra.
11. The Pateressa.

12. The Egkolpion.
13. The Manduas.
14. The Rhason.
15. The Enteri.
16. The Kalumaukion.
17. The Epanikalumaukion.

Here follows an explanation of each of these vestments in detail.

No. 1. The *Sticharion of the Priest*. This vestment is related to the *Albe* of the Western Church. It is seen in diagram at Fig. 174*a*. It is also seen in wear at Figs. 177, 180 and 181. Then also if we turn back to Figs. 171, 172 and 173 we have evidently the same garment, here bearing those longitudinal stripes—the ancient Roman *Clavi* and called by the Greeks " ποταμοί "—as a prominent feature in each case.

This *Sticharion*, in modern times, may be of any colour and is generally of silk or velvet.

The Sticharion of the Deacon is shown in diagram at Fig. 176*b*, and in wear at 179*a*.

As will be seen it has wider sleeves than the *Priest's Sticharion* but it also reaches to the feet. It is generally made of striped or brocaded silk. The diagram Fig. 176*b* is taken from a vestment now in use at the Greek Church of St. Sophia in London.

No. 2. *The Epitrachelion*. This vestment is related to the *Stole* of the Western Church and is seen in diagram at Fig. 174*f*. The two ends of the *Epitrachelion*, in modern times, are generally hooked together or sewn up, leaving a loop to go over the head. It is seen in wear at Figs. 177, 180 and 181. It is usually ornamented with crosses (*see* Fig. 174*k*) or with figures of saints and it ends in fringes. Fig. 174*f* is taken from a vestment now in use at the Greek Church of St. Sophia in London.

No. 3. *The Zone*. This is a narrow belt worn round the waist and holding together the *Epitrachelion* and *Sticharion*. It also serves as a means of suspending the *Epigonation*. It is not here illustrated though its presence can be inferred on any of the figures wearing an *Epigonation*.

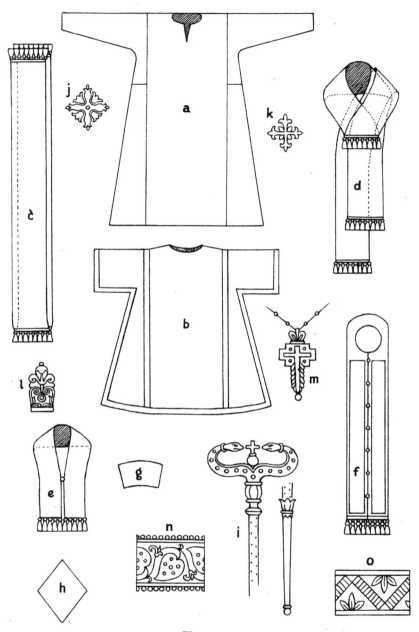

Fig. 174.

No. 4. *The Sakkos.* This vestment is very similar in shape to the *Dalmatic* of the Western Church though of totally different usage.

In the Eastern Church the *Sakkos* was originally only worn by Patriarchs but it has been worn by Bishops also since 1543.

The *Sakkos* is richly embroidered all over and the open sides are joined by either bows of ribbon, clasps or loops of cord with buttons ; these latter sometimes take the form of little bells.

The *Sakkos* is seen in diagram at Fig. 174*b*, and this has been taken from a specimen in the collections of the Victoria and Albert Museum, London. It is made from a brocaded silk of which the pattern is shown at Fig. 183, where also is seen, embroidered upon the silk so that it is upon the breast of the wearer, a roundel showing the Holy Mother and Child. The embroidered stripes which also ornament this *Sakkos* are shown, in part, at Fig. 174*o*. This vestment is shown in wear at Figs. 177 and 180.

No. 5. *The Epigonation.* This is a lozenge-shaped pendant of stiff material (often lined with cardboard). It hangs from the right side of the *Zone* as far down as the knee. It is said to have been originally a handkerchief, and so corresponds to the *Maniple* of the Western Church, where, however, it has shown a different development except in the case of the Pope of Rome alone, who wears it in the lozenge shape of the Eastern Church. This vestment is richly embroidered. In the diagram, Fig. 174*h*, the shape is given and it is seen in wear at Figs. 171 and 173, also at Figs. 177, 180 and 181.

No. 6. *The Great and Lesser Omophoria.* The *Great Omophorion* is a survival of that bordered toga characteristic

of late Roman costume and seen in its original form at
Fig. 138*a, b* and *c.*   It is also seen in its later development
on the figure of St. Agnes at Plate V*b*.   In the present
chapter it has two forms, the first of these being identical in
shape with the example seen at Plate V*b* and consisting
of a long straight band which can be seen in wear at Figs.
172 and 173, also 177 and 180.   In these four examples it
is draped over the shoulders so that one end hangs down in
front and one behind and is held thus in position by pins.

A modern form of shaping the *Great Omophorion* is shown
at diagrams 174*c* and *d.*   The vestment is here cut so that
the right side of the material is always uppermost, hence the
decoration does not need to go right through the stuff which,
in this case, is lined with plain silk while the upper side is
embroidered with crosses.   This specimen, 174*c* and *d* is
from the vestments in use at the Greek Church of St.
Sophia in London.   The *Great Omophorion* is only worn at the
Divine Liturgy until the Gospel is read.   Afterwards, at the
Celebration, it is replaced by the *Lesser Omophorion,* which
latter vestment can be seen in diagram at Fig. 174*e* ; this,
like 174*c* and *d,* is from the Greek Church of St. Sophia in
London.

The Lesser Omophorion can be seen in wear on a Bishop
of the Russian Church at Fig. 181.

No. 7. *The Epimanikia.*   These are stiff gauntlets or
cuffs, like long gloves with the hands cut off and are embroidered with crosses or holy images.   They are put on over
the sleeves of the Priests' *Sticharion.*   At first the *Epimanikia*
were worn by Bishops only, but since 1600 they have been
permitted also to Priests, though only Bishops can wear
them embroidered with the Icon of Christ.

The diagram at Fig. 174*g* shows the shape, and at

Fig. 182 a richly decorated specimen is shown which is from the collections at the Victoria and Albert Museum, London, and dating from the eighteenth century. As will be seen the embroidery has for its subject and central feature the Annunciation. Over the head of the Blessed Virgin we see the Greek Letters MP, ΘΥ., in full, MHTHP ΘEOY (Mother of God). Below, at the feet of the Virgin, there is also an inscription so defaced by time as to be indecipherable. A number of Greek letters have been assembled in the drawing, roughly resembling the old inscription so as to preserve the decorative effect of the whole design.

The *Epimanikia* will be seen in wear at Figs. 177, 181 and 182.

No. 8. *The Phenolion* corresponds to the *Chasuble* of the Western Church and, like it, is derived from that garment worn by Roman travellers which was called the *Paenula* (the Greek and Latin names show their similarity). Reference has already been made in this volume to the *Paenula* and it is seen in wear at Figs. 140 and 141.

Like the *Chasuble* of the Western Church the *Phenolion* is worn at the Celebration. While in early times this vestment in both Eastern and Western Churches was soft and voluminous and appears to have been cut on an almost circular plan; later the cut more nearly approached the semi-circular in shape.

As seen in wear at Figs. 171, 172 and 173, we have the vestment in its full, soft and apparently circular form. Though voluminous, the softness here permits of the elevation of the hands without any great difficulty, but in later times when this vestment as the *Chasuble* of the Western Church was made of stiff silk and decorated with rich embroideries which had to be displayed on a comparatively plain surface

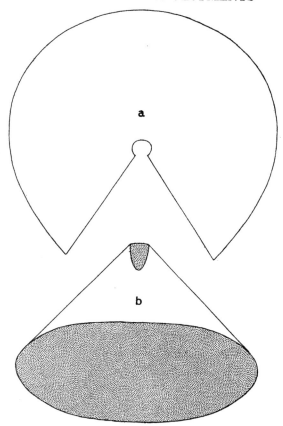

Fig. 175.

to be effective, the need arose for shortening the sides to admit of the hands being raised. This shortening gradually increased until, in the fifteenth century, we get the form known as "the fiddle-back *Chasuble*" which resembles, in silhouette, the shape of a violin.

In the Eastern Church, however, a different development took place and the *Phenolion* was shortened in front instead of at each side, so we find the form seen in diagram at Fig. 175*b*. This diagram is taken from a vestment in use at the

Greek Church of St. Sophia in London, and it is of Russian origin. The type is seen in wear at Fig. 181.

No. 9. *The Orarion.* This is, in form, a narrow band, and is worn by the clergy according to their rank. The *Orarion of the Deacon* is seen in wear at Fig. 179a (179b shows the decoration of this band). It will be noticed that the arrangement of the *Orarion* on the Deacon is not dissimilar to that seen in the arrangement of the *Stole* on a Deacon of the Western Church.

No. 10. *The Mitra.* This head-dress bears no resemblance to the *Mitre* worn by Bishops of the Western Church, and is in fact the crown of the Byzantine Emperors, which was assumed by the Patriarch of Constantinople as representing the sovereignty after the Turkish conquest in 1453. The *Mitra* is of gilded metal or of cloth of gold stretched over a metal framework and is richly decorated with jewels and holy pictures in gold and enamel.

It is seen in wear on a Bishop of the Greek Church, at Fig. 177. When this *Mitra* is compared with the crown of the Byzantine Emperor, Andronicus Palaeologus, of the late thirteenth century (*see* Fig. 166), the similarity is remarkable. Two other examples of the *Mitra* are seen at Figs. 180 and 181; these are from the Russian Church.

No. 11. *The Pateressa.* This corresponds to the *Pastoral Staff* of a Bishop of the Western Church. It is shown in use at Figs. 177 and 178a, also the detail is shown to a larger scale at Fig. 174i. It will be seen that the head of the *Pateressa* is decorated with two serpents on either side of a small cross.

No. 12. *The Egkolpion* is a pectoral cross and is seen in wear at Fig. 177 (this cross is shown to a large scale at Fig. 174m). The *Egkolpion* is also seen in wear at Figs. 178a and 181.

No. 13. *The Manduas.* This vestment is similar to the *Cope* of the Western Church. It is worn on certain occasions by the Archimandrite and the higher orders of the priesthood.

The *Manduas* is fuller than the semi-circular *Cope* of the Western Church. It is fastened in front at the lower edge as well as at the top. When worn by Bishops it is ornamented by decorative stripes. The *Manduas* is seen in diagram at Fig. 175*a*, which is taken from the collection of vestments at the Victoria and Albert Museum, London. Fig. 175*a* is from the Coptic branch of the Eastern Church and the date is nineteenth century. The *Manduas* is seen in wear on

Fig. 176.

a Bishop of the Greek Church at Fig. 178a, also a portion of the decoration of this *Manduas* is shown at Fig. 178b.

No. 14. *The Rhason.* This wide-sleeved garment has been worn by the monks of the Greek Church since the tenth century. It is of plain black cloth and is seen in wear beneath the *Manduas* at Fig. 178a. A diagram of the *Manduas* is given at Fig. 176a, and this is from the Greek Church of St. Sophia in London.

No. 15. *The Enteri.* This is a cassock-like garment of plain black cloth and is worn under the *Rhason.* It is not illustrated here.

No. 16. *The Kalumaukion,* this head-dress worn by the clergy of the Greek Church would seem to be of Asiatic origin. It is seen in wear at Figs. 176d and 179a. These two illustrations should be compared with Fig. 176f, which is from a stone relief at Persepolis and dates fifth century B.C., and the head-dress here seems to be identical in type with that worn by the Greek clergy at the present time as shown at Figs. 176d and 179a.

No. 17. *The Epanikalumaukion* or hood-like veil is worn by monks only (the higher clergy of the Greek Church—the Archimandrites, Bishops and Patriarchs are invariably monks whereas the ordinary parish Priests can marry.) This veil is seen in wear on an Archimandrite at Fig. 176d, and on a Bishop at Fig. 178a. It is also seen, in diagram, at Fig. 176c, which pattern is taken from a veil in use at the Greek Church of St. Sophia in London. It will be noticed that there are lappets attached to either side of this hooded veil and their purpose is a symbolic one, namely, for stopping the ears to shut out the noise of the world. The material of the veil at Fig. 176c is a thick black gauze.

Fig. 177.

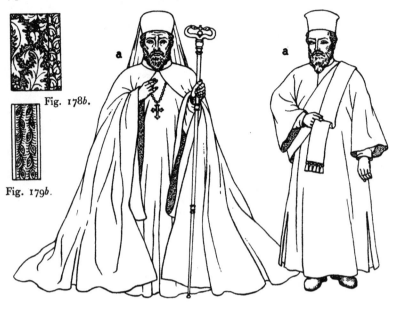

Fig. 178b.

Fig. 179b.

Fig. 178a.   Fig. 179a.

The head-dress of the Greek Bishop seen at Fig. 178a and worn under an *Epanikalumaukion* is of a different shape to that seen at Figs. 176d and 179a, but it also suggests an Oriental origin and should be compared with the drawing, Fig. 176e, which is an ancient Persian head-dress of the same date as Fig. 176f.

The foregoing list of seventeen vestments in use in the Greek Church of to-day is given for the especial purpose of comparison with Byzantine costume and described from that aspect only. There are, however, several excellent modern volumes (*see* list of works of reference) which describe the symbolism and manner of use of the vestments and also their variations according to which branch of the Eastern Church they belong.

Fig. 180.

It will be sufficient here to give a few further details of each set of vestments shown in wear from Fig. 171 to 181.

Fig. 171, to which reference has previously been made, (a Patriarch of the ninth century A.D.), is noteworthy further in two respects. Firstly, in that the decorative *Superhumeral* around the shoulders resembles to some extent that worn by the Byzantine Emperor, Andronicus Palaeologus, at Fig. 166, Chap. IV. Secondly, it should be noted that the right hand of this figure is raised to give the Blessing after the manner of the Greek Church, in which the thumb and third finger are engaged or crossed. The view of the hand, as seen at Fig. 171, explains the position of the fingers and thumb more clearly than elsewhere, as in all the other instances shown (*i.e.* Figs. 172, 173, 177 and 178*a*) the hand is in back view.

Fig. 177, a Bishop of the Greek Church is fully vested for the Divine Liturgy, whereas the Greek Bishop at Fig. 178*a* is in *Processional Dress*. Besides the Pectoral Cross or *Egkolpion*, Fig. 177 is seen to wear two pendants suspended by chains, each pendant containing a holy relic. Enlargements of the details of this elaborately ornamented set of vestments is seen at Fig. 174*j*, *l*, *m* and *n*.

Fig. 180 is a Russian Archbishop, vested, and carrying the two candlesticks. The *Trikerion* and *Dikerion* symbolizing the Holy Trinity and the dual nature of our Lord. Fig. 181, a Russian Bishop, vested for the Divine Liturgy, has the hands merely raised, not giving the Blessing, in this case, of the Greek ritual. The remaining vestments have already been sufficiently described as has also the ornament.

Fig. 181.

Fig. 182.

Fig. 183.

BIBLIOGRAPHY

CHAPTER I. AEGEAN COSTUME

Annual of the British School at Athens, vols. vii. to xi., inclusive.

Baikie, *Sea Kings of Crete.*

Bossert, *Alt Kreta.*

Botsford, *Hellenic History,* 1922.

Burn, *Minoans, Philistines and Greeks,* 1930.

Cambridge Ancient History, 1927.

Childe, *The Most Ancient East,* 1929.

Cotteril, *History of Art,* 1922.

Della Seta, *Religion and Art,* 1914.

Evans, *The Palace of Minos,* 1921–36.

Glotz, *The Aegean Civilization,* 1925.

Hagia Triada, Para beni Rendiconti, vol. xiii.

Hall, E. H., *The Decorative Art of Crete in the Bronze Age.*

Hall, H. R., *Aegean Archaeology,* 1915.

Hall, H. R., *Ancient History of the Near East,* 1913.

Hawes, *Gournia,* 1901–4.

Loeschcke, *Tiryns II.,* Kaiserlich Deutsches, 1912, Tafel viii.

Minns, *Scythians and Greeks,* 1913.

Monumenti Antichi, vols. xiii. and xix ; *Reale Academia dei Lincei,* 1908.

Mosso, *The Palaces of Crete.*

Myres, *The Dawn of History.*

Pseira, Philadelphia University, *Anthropologia,* No. 3, 1910.

Rostovtzeff, *History of the Ancient World,* 1926.

Schliemann, *Mycenae,* 1878.

Spearing, *The Childhood of Art,* 1912.

CHAPTER II. ANCIENT GREEK COSTUME

Abrahams, *Greek Dress*, 1908.

Bossert, *Ornament* (for decoration only).

Botsford, *Hellenic History*, 1922.

British Museum Guide-books and Postcards.

Cambridge Ancient History, 1927.

Carotti (trans. de Zoete), *History of Art*, 1909.

Cotteril, *History of Art*, 1922.

Della Seta, *Religion and Art*, 1914.

Evans (Lady), *Chapters on Greek Dress*, 1893.

Fürtwangler, *Griechische Vase Malerei*, 1904.

Gardner, E. A., *Art of Greece*, 1915.

Gardner, P., *Grammar of Greek Art*, 1905.

Glotz, *Ancient Greeks at Work*, 1926.

Heuzey, *Histoire du Costume Antique*, 1922.

Hope, *Costume of the Ancients*, 1841.

Hottenroth, *Le Costume*, 1896.

Lübke (trans. Sturgis), *Outline of the History of Art*, 1904.

Minns, Ellis Hovel, *Scythians and Greeks*, 1913.

Nettleship and Sandys, *Dictionary of Classical Antiquities*, 1891.

von Reber, *History of Ancient Art*, 1883.

Rostovtzeff, *History of the Ancient World*, 1926.

Smith, *Dictionary of Greek and Roman Antiquities*, 1901.

Walters, *A Classical Dictionary*, 1916.

CHAPTER III. ANCIENT ROMAN COSTUME

British Museum Guide-books and Postcards.

Cambridge Ancient History, 1927.

Cambridge Companion to Latin Studies, 1929.

Carotti (trans. de Zoete), *History of Art*, 1909.

Cotteril, *History of Art*, 1922.

Della Seta, *Religion and Art*, 1914.

Ferrero, *Women of the Caesars*, 1911.

Forestier, *The Roman Soldier*.

Heuzey, *Histoire du Costume Antique*, 1922.

Hope, *Costume of the Ancients*, 1841.

Lübke (trans. Sturgis), *Outline of the History of Art*, 1904.

Nettleship and Sandys, *Dictionary of Classical Antiquities*, 1891.

Poulsen, *Etruscan Tomb Paintings*, 1922.

von Reber, *History of Ancient Art*, 1883.
Rostovtzeff, *History of the Ancient World : Rome*, 1927.

Smith, *Dictionary of Greek and Roman Antiquities*, 1901.
Strong, *Art in Ancient Rome*, 1929.
Strong, *Roman Sculpture*, 1907.

Walters, *A Classical Dictionary*, 1916.
Weege, *Etruskischen Malerei*, 1921.
Wulff and Volbach, *Spätantike und Koptische Stoff*, 1926 (for ornament only).

CHAPTER IV. BYZANTINE COSTUME

Anthony, E. W., *History of Mosaics*, 1935.

Bock, *Die Kleinodien des Heiligen Römischen Reiches*, 1864.
British Museum, *Collections and Photographs*.

Carotti, *A History of Art* (trans. de Zoete), 1909.
Colasanti, *L'Arte Bisantina in Italia*, 1912.
Cotteril, *A History of Art* (2 vols.), vol. i, 1922.

Dalton, *British Museum Guide to Early Christian and Byzantine Antiquities*, 1921.
Dalton, *Byzantine Art and Archaeology*, 1911.
Deihl, *Manuel d'Art Byzantin*, 1921.
Della Seta, *Religion and Art*, 1914.

Jacquemin, *Iconographie*, 1867.

Michel, *Histoire de l'Art*, vol. i, 1905.

Rice, *Byzantine Art*, 1935.
Rossi, *Musaici Cristiani delli Chiese di Roma*, 1899.

Venturi, *History of Italian Art*, 1926.
Victoria and Albert Museum, *Collections and Photographs*.

Wilpert, *Die Römischen Mosaiken und Malerei (fourth to thirteenth century)*, 1917.

CHAPTER V. THE VESTMENTS OF THE EASTERN ORTHODOX CHURCH

Braun, *Die Liturgische Gewandung*, 1907.

Dalton, O. M., *Byzantine Art and Archaeology*, 1911.

Dalton, O. M., *Early Christian Art*, 1925.

Douglas, Rev. J. A., *Pictures of Russian Worship*, 1915.

Douglas, Rev. J. A., *The Sacraments in Russia*, 1915.

Fortescue, Rev. Adrian, *The Orthodox Eastern Church*, 1929.

Hottenroth, *Le Costume*, 1896.

Janin, R., Les églises separées d'Orient, 1930.

Macalister, R. A. S., *Ecclesiastical Vestments*, 1896.

Racinet, *Le Costume*, 1888.

Romanoff, H. C., *Sketches of the Rites and Customs of the Graeco-Russian Church*, 1868.

PLATE 1.— A CRETAN COSTUME.
From a Pottery Statuette in the British Museum.